Hot Coals of Fire
The Sanctity of the Ministry

Stephen John Goundry

authorHOUSE

AuthorHouse™
1663 Liberty Drive
Bloomington, IN 47403
www.authorhouse.com
Phone: 1 (800) 839-8640

Published by AuthorHouse   11/11/2016

ISBN: 978-1-5246-4872-5 (sc)
ISBN: 978-1-5246-4871-8 (e)

Library of Congress Control Number: 2016918646

Print information available on the last page.

Any people depicted in stock imagery provided by Thinkstock are models, and such images are being used for illustrative purposes only. Certain stock imagery © Thinkstock.

This book is printed on acid-free paper.

To my loving daughter Rachel,
A holy woman of God

Contents

Foreword...ix

Introduction xiii

The Authority of the Holy Spirit 1

Blood, Fire and Water.. 13

Cloths of Service.. 26

The Anointing Oil 38

For Jesus' Sake... 48

The Fear that is Good... 56

Nobility in the Ministry 67

Lessons from a rogue Minister.. 79

Rejected Ministers 91

The Men of Anathoth..107

Saul's Spear..117

Playing the Fool 130

Tell it not in Gath..143

The Secrets of God 150

Closing Thoughts 160

Foreword

It is with much trepidation that I have written this book, simply because of the subject matter. The Scriptures often tell us to 'take heed to ourselves' because we are all 'prone to wander; prone to leave the God we love' and I am no exception. In light of this there is a part of me that would prefer to leave a book like this to others but when you have a sense that the Lord desires for you to do something, obedience is not just a good response; it's the only response. Like the soldier who has just received his orders, we too must respond willingly, saying "Yes, Sir!"

The apostle Paul told Timothy (and therefore us) that in the Last Days, perilous times would come and that evil men and imposters will grow worse and worse. The Lord Jesus also told us that lawlessness will then abound to such a point where the love of many of His own people will grow cold. We are now seeing Christian virtues and ministry standards eroding at an alarming pace, bringing great reproach upon Christ and the Christian community. If higher levels of morality are still expected of our politicians, how much more the very Ministers of Christ! Of all people, the Ministers of God should exemplify the standards set by the Master and be able to reflect His character to His people and to the world.

To those whom God calls to be His Ministers, He gives the grace to accomplish their work for Him. This extra grace upon their lives is to help balance out the requirement on them to live to higher standards than others. This requirement can be found in the high expectations that reside in the hearts and minds of people; where they can legitimately expect the best of personal behavior from those who hold ministerial office.

There are some would-be Ministers who understand this and it causes them to retreat from their callings, so as to preserve themselves from the close inspection and judgement of people. While this understandable it is not acceptable to God for a person to run away from their ministry call. I fear that they will find themselves in the unenviable position of the wicked servant who hid his talent in the ground and like him; they too will be without excuse when their Lord returns.

Then there are people who have taken up the call of ministry and they have persuaded themselves that if they should morally fail; that they will be dealt with by God the way He deals with everyone else. In this they are *greatly* mistaken, for 'to whom much is given, from him will much be required; and to whom much has been committed, of him will they ask the more.' James, in his epistle clearly warned us that those who teach will receive a stricter judgment.

The purpose of writing this book is to encourage those who ought to be obedient to their ministry calling and to warn those who are in Christian ministry to be careful in how they live, for the glory of God is at stake.

And Moses said to Aaron, "This is what the Lord spoke, saying:

'By those who come near Me I must be regarded as holy;
And before all the people I must be glorified.'"

Leviticus 10:3

Introduction

There are many topics that are covered in the chapters of this book but the message that runs through them all is the necessity of giving glory to God and that glory is predicated upon the regard that men have for the Holy Spirit. The work of Christ which includes all of redemptive history is *His* business and therefore successful ministry can only be accomplished when *He* is in charge of it!

Just as the body without the human spirit is dead, so the ministry of the Body of Christ is dead without the life-giving force of the Holy Spirit. Without Him we can do nothing of any consequence in the kingdom of God!

To this notion, most present day Ministers will give mental assent and even voice their acceptance of it and yet in many ways, if not in all their ways, seek to perform their sacred duties without Him! Consequently, the Holy Spirit will either leave or become a poor second to the 'spirit of man' who has for his own reasons, taken ownership of the *Lord's* work. This is impudence of the highest degree. To relegate God in His own work is an effrontery to Him and to ignore His *voice* which has said "Not by might, nor by power, but by My Spirit" is deeply grieving.

How did we become so spiritually dull and so careless to think that we can touch the 'ark of God' and figuratively 'walk in front of it' as if we owned it? Why do we not understand that those who minister *at* the 'altar' are handling the hot coals from *off* it? What is it about our attitudes to-day that allows us to be so elevated within ourselves, that we don't see how rude we've become and how, even as Ministers, we have insulted the Spirit of Grace through His exclusion?

As usual, there is a path to every kind of behavior and as an introduction to the subsequent chapters in this book; I'd like to take a look at the historical roots of our attitudes to-day. By tracing the cultural influences of previous generations, we will see both the good and the bad concerning the shaping of our present day values.

I think that it can be safely said that previous generations would blush at what they would see now. They would sincerely wonder how such a slide in standards could happen in such a short time. It's not that they themselves were without sin, but their lives were lived under higher codes of behavior underscored by Christian beliefs and influence. They did not know the excesses of our day but the 'leaven' *was* in the lump and it was only a matter of time before the ethics that kept former societies together would be viewed as barriers to personal freedom. In the process of time, the 'leaven' of sin has risen up to give mankind an over-exalted view of itself.

Let us ask ourselves a couple of questions. Firstly, how did we become who we are? Secondly, what have been the cultural influences that have colored our world-views; developed our thoughts and shaped our way of life? The answer to understanding the 'spirit of man' to-day is found in the roots of our Western culture. One of the problems that the Church in the west has had over many centuries stems from the fact that the Bible is a Middle-Eastern book. Even in the cosmopolitan world of our times, while humanity retains its universal aspects, Middle-Eastern and Far-Eastern thought is clearly not ours. So if *our* mind-set is not from *those* regions of the world, where is it from?

History gives us the answer to this question and the ones previously asked.

Our mind-set to-day largely comes from the Greek civilization. The Romans 'came onboard' shall we say, but it was Greek philosophy; Greek culture; Greek politics; Greek mathematics; Greek science; Greek theater; Greek art, etc., that was embraced. It was a culture that had lost its inherent regard for the One True God and yet it was full of other gods and the sexual immorality that always accompanies such idolatry. Individualism was a cornerstone to their way of life in which a political process called democracy gave to man the privileges and the responsibilities of a vote. (In the realm of the human, democracy is the fairest way to govern but in the kingdom of God the Lord is King and theocracy is the way things are done. 'The government is upon *His* shoulder.' Theocracy glorifies God and His chosen representatives. Democracy glorifies man and His elected representatives.)

Simply put, Greek culture elevates man. That is why they were obsessed with the acquisition of wisdom. Like Eve in the Garden of Eden, they reached out for that which could make them wise.

After the Classical worlds of the Greek and Roman empires, a spiritual and an intellectual darkness came and so began the so-called 'Middle Ages.'

The Middle Ages, also known as the Dark Ages dominated the Western world for centuries. Where had all that Greek culture gone? It went to the center of the Eastern Roman empire. It found a home in Constantinople and there it remained in both the civil and religious life of the city until the fall of its 'Christian kingdom' in the fifteenth century. The Islamic spirit came in and the Greek spirit flew to Western Europe for refuge. The people who carried that Greek culture arrived in Italy at an opportune time and they greatly contributed to the ongoing rebirth of Europe. It became known as the Renaissance which was the rebirth and revival of classic Greek and Roman culture.

The whole movement was seen as a coming out of the darkness of ignorance and religious superstition into the light of knowledge. This confluence of events came at a ripe time in the hearts of men because they had grown weary of the overbearing, unaccountable authority of the Mediaeval Church and they were tired of being the 'little guy' groveling at the feet of priests and kings; both of whom derived their power from the Church.

Now, a 'new wind' was blowing and it was intoxicating for the masses. Now, the 'little guy' could become the 'big guy' if he could get the power. Now, the 'little guy' didn't need to be born into aristocracy or have the peculiar sanctions of the Church; now all he needed was the money!

This was the time when many merchant families arose to great wealth and power. Notable families like the Medici's found that they could make more money with loans and with credits than by practicing medicine. The family of the Medici's became the single most influential power during the Renaissance.

From this time forward, with a revival of the 'spirit of man' who was now drinking deeply from the fountain of Greek philosophy, man was on his own way to glory. By embracing the non-religious, non-Church world of the ancient Greeks, man could make his own way in the world. The Renaissance with its deep vein of classical Greek culture was seen as a break from the past; a break from Church monopoly and a break from kings and their feudal barons.

For most people this was a welcome break and a departing from those institutions was not without some justification.

So, Europe entered the world of the individual to where even city-states with great commercial strength had more power than some countries. Now, it didn't matter what birth you had because the individual could by wit, stealth, energy and industry become what he always wanted – the 'big guy.'

(For centuries then, we've all been on a journey which can be called the 'ascent of man' and Greek culture has aided and abetted us all.)

It wasn't long before monarchs had to yield to the will of their populations and where parliaments everywhere were beginning the arduous journey of governing their constituents over and against the kings ruling their subjects. The good thing about this era for the true Christian believers in many countries was that the Holy Scriptures came to them in their own languages. The stranglehold of the mediaeval Church in this matter was broken and a reformation of true Christian doctrine took place. Now the 'little guy' could become a Minister of Christ. The prerequisites for a Ministry vocation became more spiritual than political and while education remained a part of the training process, the essentials of God's calling and anointing were esteemed once more. The 'wind of change' had not only blown away the encumbrances of the past; it had also blown open new doors of opportunity for the common man. For all the good and bad that came with this 'wind' it was as they say, a 'breath of fresh air' for the majority.

With the 'spirit of man' now riding high in the world, another 'child' was born and her name was 'Enlightenment.' As she grew she appealed greatly to the forward-thinking nations of Europe and they fell in love with her, worshiping her for the knowledge she offered them. This was a religion for man by man. It was called 'Individualism.' It proffered the elevation of man to the dizzy heights of self-glorification and so the modern day 'self-made man' was born.

Philosophers in France, Britain and Germany began to promote man and his powers of reason, of logic, and of science as the way forward. They didn't want to be shackled to an out of date Christian religion; especially one that seemed to come second to science. Consequently, the pride of man became puffed up with his discoveries, with his explorations and with his own rationale. Concurrently, there was a revival in Greek architecture and art with many of their new public buildings showing Greek design. Edinburgh in Scotland was known as the 'Athens of the North.' In the United States, Greek culture and Greek architectural design found a very comfortable place because Greek style buildings gave the appearance of grandeur without religious authority or overtones. Like the Freemasons of their time, they would be happy to build temples on the scale of Solomon, but the God of Solomon would not be found in them!

History has proven that when man wants to be his own god, he has to extinguish the old one. Consequently, there came great debating over the veracity of the Bible. Those who didn't downright reject it fused its truths with other ancient writings and then Christ was seen on par with Aristotle, Plato and Seneca, etc. The whole era brought ancient Greece back to its former pre-eminence–a world of many gods – "Pick the ones that *you* like! It's all up to you! You're in charge now. Life is what *you* make it!" Such is the seductive power of Athena, the goddess of wisdom.

While many of these things ignited personal freedom they also spawned an unhealthy self-exaltation in man which when its full rotten fruit became ripe, created horror in the world through wildly ambitious men producing a personality cult around themselves. Napoleon Bonaparte; Adolf Hitler; Joseph Stalin; Benito Mussolini, Mao Zedong; Saddam Hussein all elevated themselves in their generations– and the world wept.

These of course are extreme examples but there have been more insidious effects of Greek philosophy that have come upon us. While we can be thankful for the freedoms and the protections that we now enjoy we must still weigh everything in the balances of true discernment. On the one hand, we can be grateful for its political influence in that we do enjoy certain rights; we do have representation and the vote. We can be grateful that the religious and political grip of the Church has been broken and that kings and queens can no longer execute us at their whim. But on the other hand there are some deep things to deal with because there is now pressure upon the individual as never before. In olden times you weren't expected to achieve for yourself; you were expected to do your part in keeping the manor going for the lord and master. Because of the elevation of man we're now *expected* to be successful individuals. This notion of personal success has become deep-seated in the lives of all of us and as a consequence, the need to get and keep one's success has proved to be a life-trap for many. This expectation for each one to be successful comes from the inside motivations of the human heart and the outside influences of present-day society. Expectation *by* the individual and *upon* the individual has become an 'iron suit' and many are finding it difficult if not impossible to 'swim.'

For the Christian whose caught between a 'walk with God' and the need to produce and excel, it sometimes proves a 'bridge too far.'

For Christian Ministers who are now required to produce tangible, measurable results, they also can find the burden of high expectation too much to carry. Today's philosophical messages of self-empowerment, self-enhancement and personal freedom are being fed into us from centuries of a revived, ancient godless culture and we've 'bought into it.' Why wouldn't we? It's selling everything we're personally looking for! However, the messages today if not properly discerned can promote us in an unhealthy way. That which liberated us during the Renaissance might have been good for us then but our sinful natures have caused it to turn on us and is now eating us!

We are now found worshiping the worst of idols and that is the idol of 'self.'

We have conveniently forgotten the Holy Scriptures which tells us that promotion comes from the Lord; that God is the Judge of all men and that He puts down one and exalts another! Back in the Garden of Eden, Eve tried to promote herself and consequently her life fell apart. She wasn't content with all the things that God had given her and in a spirit of rebellion through self-promotion, she came under the judgment of God. The Lord is not against the progress of man -He's against the self-glorification of man. *God* is the 'Big Guy' in that sense and we do well to remember that man is man and God is God! We must be careful not allow centuries of constantly hearing how good and how great mankind is to deceive us.

Please don't allow those messages to mislead you. Please don't be fooled and become wise in your own conceits, but consider Almighty God. Consider giving *Him* the glory. We are at our happiest when we glorify God. A Minister is at his or her happiest when they do everything for the glory of God and have learned how to honor and work with His Holy Spirit. How gracious God is to allow the world to reject

Him even though His arms of love are open to them every day and how gracious God is to His Ministers when they replace Him with their own selves and endeavor to do the work of God without Him!

The Authority of the Holy Spirit

It seems fitting to begin this first chapter with the Holy Spirit of God because He is always at the front and center of everything God does and it is *His* absence that causes us to forget the sanctity of the ministry. It's His Presence that causes us to walk very carefully before a holy God and to treat His things with reverence and respect.

Let's begin with the basics. Who is the Holy Spirit and what does He do?

The Holy Spirit is a Divine Person. He is *God* the Holy Spirit and He is the Third Person of the Trinity. The Bible reveals that the Godhead consists of the Father, the Son and the Holy Spirit. The Father and the Son are in heaven but they are both operating in the earth through the Holy Spirit. Their authority is revealed in the earth through the agency of the Holy Spirit, and that's why the Holy Spirit is the true 'vicar of Christ' on earth. He is the true representative of God in the world and of Christ in the Church. In the world, it is the Holy Spirit that restrains evil, bringing judgment on both people and nations when their sins have reached up to heaven. He is the One who keeps the spirit of 'antichrist' in chains of restriction and stops us all from annihilating each other.

Ultimately, it's *His* finger on the 'button.' He's the One in charge of history and in particular, 'redemptive history' which means that He is the custodian of the purposes of God among the elect; among those in every generation who will be saved. That also means that He is in charge of the ministry. He's in charge of the missions program of God.

He calls - He sends
Acts 13:1-4

'Now in the church that was at Antioch there were certain prophets and teachers: Barnabas, Simeon who was called Niger, Lucius of Cyrene, Manaen who had been brought up with Herod the tetrarch, and Saul.

As they ministered to the Lord and fasted, the Holy Spirit said, "Now separate to Me Barnabas and Saul for the work to which I have called them."

Then, having fasted and prayed, and laid hands on them, they sent them away.

So, being sent out by the Holy Spirit, they went down to Seleucia, and from there they sailed to Cyprus.'

Here we see how much the Holy Spirit is in control of the ministry. What you have here is what is known as a 'governmental prophecy' where certain individuals are set apart by the Holy Spirit for *ministry office* through the voice of a prophet or prophets.

(There are some dangers to this level of prophesying. Prophets can get it wrong or even abuse it and send somebody in the wrong direction, but the secret of safety is in the words recorded here. The Holy Spirit said, *"Separate to Me now, Barnabas and Saul for the work to which I have called them."* Before there is a 'sending' there is always a 'calling.' God is not going to send an individual anywhere where He hasn't already spoken to them about it in their hearts.

Barnabas and Saul had been waiting on the Holy Spirit for this very moment, and it was confirmed through prophecy at that meeting.)

V4 – *'So they, being sent out by the Holy Spirit.….'*

The commencement of the ministry of Barnabas and Saul was both planned and sanctioned by none other than the Holy Spirit of God. He was the One in charge of their calling and their sending and because they were obedient to Him, their ministry together knew great power and great timing.

The end of Acts chapter fourteen tells us of their triumphant return to the church at Antioch from where they had first received their commission.

Acts 14:26-27

'From there they sailed to Antioch, where they had been commended to the grace of God for the work which they had completed.

Now when they had come and gathered the church together, they reported all that God had done with them, and that He had opened the door of faith to the Gentiles.'

They were called by the Holy Spirit; set apart by the Holy Spirit; anointed by the Holy Spirit; sent out by the Holy Spirit and used by the Holy Spirit!

This is how Christian ministry *should* be done. *This is true ministry.* This is the ministry that will be judged by Jesus to be like gold, silver and precious jewels.

This kind of work, done this kind of way, will know God's approval forever.

This is the *only* way to be truly effective in the world and when you work for God *this* way, heaven will always support you for 'where God guides, there He provides.'

Let's take a look at another example of the Holy Spirit being in charge of the missionary program of the Church.

Acts 16:6-10

'Now when they had gone through Phrygia and the region of Galatia, they were forbidden by the Holy Spirit to preach the word in Asia.

After they had come to Mysia, they tried to go into Bithynia, but the Spirit did not permit them.

So passing by Mysia, they came down to Troas.

And a vision appeared to Paul in the night. A man of Macedonia stood and pleaded with him, saying, "Come over to Macedonia and help us."

Now after he had seen the vision, immediately we sought to go to Macedonia, concluding that the Lord had called us to preach the gospel to them.'

This is a great example of the Holy Spirit exercising His authority in the Church of Christ and in the lives of His Ministers. The disciples desired to preach the word in the province of Asia, but the Holy Spirit forbade them to go there. He wouldn't permit it. He stopped them going in that direction because it wasn't His will. Then the disciples tried to go into the region of Bithynia, but once again, the Holy Spirit didn't allow them to go there either. It was no doubt a little confusing for them, but clarity came when the Holy Spirit gave Paul a vision in the night of a man from Macedonia and they knew then, that they must preach the word *there*. And so the Gospel went west–into Europe. And the rest as they say "is history."

Let's take a look at one more example of the authority of the Holy Spirit being exercised in the ministry of the Church.

He Leads - He guides
Galatians 2:1-2

'Then after fourteen years I went up again to Jerusalem with Barnabas, and also took Titus with me. And I went up by revelation,

4

and communicated to them that gospel which I preach among the Gentiles, but privately to those who were of reputation, lest by any means I might run, or had run, in vain.'

The Apostle Paul didn't just decide in himself that it was time he paid a visit to the leaders of the church in Jerusalem. He said that his decision to go there was a result of a revelation from the Holy Spirit. *"I went up by revelation"* he said. The Holy Spirit sent him there. This is how true ministry is done. It's all done under the auspices of the Holy Spirit and therefore it's about what *He* wants and not what *we* would like!

Who wouldn't want to have a 'walk with God' like this? Sadly, it's at this very point where many Christians and many Christian Ministers part ways with Him simply because *we* want to do what *we* want to do and *we* want to do it *when* we want to do it! In other words, there comes a clash of wills.

And when the supernatural element of God is no longer expected or even required, it just becomes easier for us to do the ministry without Him. It is the 'individual' who now wants to be in charge. We want to be in control of things. We want to manage our time and manage the work. In a generation such as ours, waiting *on* God and *for* God becomes very frustrating and quite boring. There's a desire and a need in us to 'get the job done' and so it's difficult to wait at the gate when all you want to do is run the race! Also, there are many deep personal costs to walking with God. Now if our hearts truly love God none of these things are too heavy for us, because at the end of the day, we just want God's will to be done. And so we will happily wait; we will joyfully obey and we will be content to let Him be in control of our lives.

Alas, not everybody's heart is like this. Many don't want to 'take up their cross daily' and so they find themselves subtly resisting the Holy Spirit's authority in their lives. They know the Bible but they don't comply with its commands and so they limp along in their Christian lives, professing Christ yet quenching His Spirit. They think they have enough 'juice' to get by, but they find it increasingly difficult to live the Christian life because they've lost a vital connection and they've pulled their own 'plug out of the socket.' The sad result of all that is a weakened Church which has no real authority in the world. There is no 'shout of a king amongst us' and the world can only see us as a bunch of 'do-gooders.' If convictions such as these are absent in the Ministers of the Church, how can there be any in the world? Why should they listen to *us*?

I think that the Church down through the centuries has inwardly known that its vitality rests in the Holy Spirit, but it hasn't stopped us pushing Him out. Oh yes, we all like Him when He comes as the great Comforter, but when He comes as the great Disturber, He is shown the door. And then the Lord has the embarrassment of saying to us the Church, *"Behold, I stand at the door and knock."*

The Holy Spirit and the truths of Scripture have been evicted many, many times, and He has been replaced by our own energies and designs.

Let me now share with you what we've done over the years. To Europeans, 200 miles is a long way and to Americans, 200 years is a long time. Because I hale from England, I'd like to go back about 200 years and hopefully show you some of the ways in which we have during that short period of time grieved the Holy Spirit and even replaced Him with ourselves on many occasions.

Quenching the Spirit

In the introduction of this book the path to man's self-glorification was seen in its historical context. When the era of man's 'enlightenment' came into bloom, the Church began to lose its influence on people because it was an 'age of reason' and the supernatural elements of the Bible were scorned. The Church began to combat its detractors by getting Christian men of great intellect to produce a system of arguments and apologetics in defense of the Faith; hoping to restore and establish the Christian faith –rationally. They tried to win their opponents by debate.

That approach didn't restore the Church's authority at that time so what did? It was the spiritual revivals through people like John Wesley and George Whitfield, who preached the Gospel with signs following. God restored the Church's influence in the world and He brought it about in His own way -the Biblical way! There were things that happened in those spiritual revival meetings that defied reason and they discovered the fact that the supernatural working of God cannot easily be explained.

Throughout the centuries the Church has met the derision of the world with everything but the fire of God. When the Holy Spirit is virtually absent the real tools to get the job done are simply not there. All that is left is our best efforts which will never prove sufficient to advance the kingdom of God.

The Church leadership in many generations has tried to come up with solutions to its lack of impact in an ever-increasing skeptical world but the spiritual revivals in America, Northern Ireland and Wales were brought about by God the Holy Spirit acting sovereignly again. Whole communities were brought under great conviction of sin as the people of God swelled all the once-forgotten prayer meetings. Church attendance increased exponentially and the Gospel that saves men's souls was preached with fire! Many supernatural signs were experienced and great miracles of healing took place because the Holy Spirit was present through His gifts.

The people who were involved in all this 'outpouring of the Holy Spirit' abandoned themselves to its powerful effects and didn't care too much how they were viewed by others as long as God received the glory.

Unfortunately, that willingness to give up the 'pride of life' receded and it wasn't too long before the people of God lost the Presence of God again.

One of the main ways that the Holy Spirit found Himself a poor second came when we adopted a deep concern for respectability in our lives and in our services. With the 'pride of life' now running high in the generation, it was seen as a time to bring a sense of dignity to the ministry of Christ.

The old-style preaching that brought both the fear and the love of God to bear upon the soul was relegated as people increasingly wanted an educated ministry. The emphasis shifted from a Minister with the anointing of the Holy Spirit upon him to a Minister who had received the best of religious education. Consequently, the Minister's intellect became more important than the Minister's heart; his schooling more than his conversion; and his qualifications more than his walk with God. As a result, the Church and its Ministers began to pay more and more attention to its liturgical forms, rituals and ceremonies.

(There's nothing wrong with the desire for a cultured, educated ministry as long as it serves the spiritual aspects of the anointing of the Holy Spirit!)

Another reason why the desire for respectability got such a stronghold in the Church was because there was in some quarters a fear of excesses in enthusiasm. In their defense the movements that did place an emphasis on the Person and work of the Holy Spirit were slated for their lack of control and sometimes, bizarre behavior. Sadly, in many cases, the criticism was fair. Many denominations of the Church during that time would have nothing to do with those 'revival fires' and have no dealings with the Ministers involved. Sadly, they quenched the Holy Spirit in their own ministries and subsequently their authority and their influence in the world diminished further. When the 'spirit of man' rejects the Spirit of God, a huge spiritual vacuum is created and to make up that ever-widening gap, men try to do the ministry their own way –which never works. When the Ministers of Christ have lost the Spirit of God they are consigned to 'walk as mere men.' The apostles who 'turned the world upside down' were men of the Spirit! It's God who is the 'game-changer' –not us! To quote the words of Jesus: *"Without Me you can do nothing."*

When we don't seek or come under the authority of the Holy Spirit we are fighting a battle that we will never win, no matter how hard we try. Without Him we will be left with only man-made ideas as to how to make the Church and its message relevant. However, that which originates with man can easily be dismissed by man; but that which begins with God is not easily dismissed by man. When the Holy Spirit is on the word, that message becomes the 'Sword of the Spirit' and when it is spoken, it runs right through the hearts of people! Sometimes, God will *not* be ignored!

All efforts to revive the work of God without God are futile. The Church can advertise all it wants. It can hire publicists to ensure exposure in the media. It can divert its efforts into showing more social concern and champion great causes for justice. It can sit on the debating stage with atheists, and show them how intellectual and scientific we are. We can even put all our once held dear doctrines aside and create a World Church so as to speak with one unified voice to every continent. As the 'spirit of man' has ascended the work of God in most places of the Western world has descended; and most Christians can see before their eyes the prophesied 'falling away.'

Entertain us or die!

The Church in this part of the world has lost nearly all its 'salt and light' now. *We're* the ones teaching folks how to be successful in life; how to make money and live the good life. As for our praise and worship, the Gospel went 'pop' decades ago. We don't need the 'lads from Liverpool' anymore to influence the music scene because we can set some of the music trends of the world on our own now! We've been giving our choir boys and our choir girls to the world for years, from Elvis Presley and Johnny Cash all the way to the present day. *We've* got the rhythms now and yes, we've got the volume and the dark auditoriums to match. It's 'lights out in the sanctuary' now. (The Church has worshiped in the light since its inception, but apparently we now know better!)

In the age in which we live, people don't flock to their local churches. Now they flock to celebrations, to festivals, to conferences, to concerts, 'gigs' and 'happenings.' Whole industries have sprung up around religiously themed entertainment and the cash for the recordings, the DVD's, the posters and the T-shirts just keeps rolling in. To meet the needs of the present generation, to-day's Church has to be 'cool' and the advertising schemes that we practiced in the early 1900's have now evolved into 'the branding of our ministries.'

The message the world gives the Church in our generation is simply this: *Entertain us or die!* The complaint used to be – "Are you preaching at me?" The complaint now is: "Why aren't you entertaining me? I'm not sitting here bored when there's a 'cool' church down the street with hundreds of young people!"

All of these things are signs to let us know that we're at the end of the Western way of life as we know it, because it mirrors the last days of a once great empire. Before Rome fell, all that the people wanted was food and entertainment. "Bread and Games – give us bread and games." I always remember the scene in the movie 'Gladiator' when Maximus stood in the arena, having won his fight, he cried out to the crowd, "Are you not entertained?"

The Church situation to-day shows us that *we have not lost touch with the world but that we have lost touch with God!* All these alternatives that have captured our endeavors down through the centuries *cannot* replace the Holy Spirit and His anointing and His authority in the ministry of the Church. And many of God's people have got to make their minds up whether they want the truth or the tune! They have to decide whether they are going to church to worship the Savior or they are going to worship the worship! Are they singing to lift Jesus higher or to make them feel better through a worship experience?

The questions for this generation all surround the sufficiency of Jesus to satisfy the soul. Is having the Lord in their life enough? Would they attend a local church if the only attraction there was God? I believe that the Holy Spirit's authority will be restored to us when we can truthfully answer "Yes" to both those questions. May God have mercy on us in this very important matter. Christ *is* our life and that life is in His Spirit –the Holy Spirit. When He is pushed out, the world seeps in and eventually takes His place. That's why the sad statistics of the world are about the same as those who profess to be Christians for if we adopt show business techniques can we be surprised if we get show business values? When the Church at large loses the sanctifying power of the Sanctified Spirit the lines of demarcation between the 'saved' and the 'unsaved' become blurry. The 'spirit of man' usurps the 'throne' and the people of God are taken with the same self-promoting ambitions as their counterparts in the world –both are living for 'the here and now.' When this happens a distinct lack of 'other worldliness' creeps in and the focus changes from a 'home up in heaven' to a 'big house down here.' Neither the 'big house' nor any other form of earthly success is the problem –it's the focus! *'For where you treasure is, there your heart will be also.'*

To honor the Father is to honor the Son and to honor them both is to honor the Spirit whom they sent to us. They are the One's in charge!

Blood, Fire and Water

Many years ago, when I lived in England, I visited a local Salvation Army Hall and I couldn't help noticing the three words that were written in large letters all the way across the platform, in front of the pulpit. The words were: 'Blood; Fire; Water.' It was an appropriate setting for such a succinct message because these three words describe the very elements of our salvation. Blood, fire and water are the purging, cleansing, sanctifying elements of a holy God. Let's take a closer look at these cleansing agents and let us begin with the first one – the blood.

The Blood of the Covenant
Leviticus 17:11

'For the life of the flesh is in the blood, and I have given it to you upon the altar to make atonement for your souls; for it is the blood that makes atonement for the soul.'

In a day where we'd rather view our sinful nature in the context of personal problems or issues, the Scriptures send out a trumpet blast in that it is our *sins* that have separated us from God and that the *blood* is the only way to atone for them. The blood is for *our* sins. It's our sins that bring us the problems and cause the issues in our lives!

From the beginning; from the sacrificial lambs of Abel's flock to the very blood of Christ, God has spoken clearly about this most essential of matters. Atonement for sins comes through the innocent life's blood of 'another' sprinkled upon the altar for our sakes. When the Bible talks about the blood, it is speaking of a life given to death instead of the guilty one and the proof of that death is in the spilt blood. All through the Scriptures, it is manifestly shown that atonement for sin was very costly.

King David knew this principle well, for when he was offered the threshing floor of Ornan the Jebusite and his oxen to boot, he flatly refused them saying. *"I will not offer burnt offerings to the Lord my God with that which costs me nothing!"* So David paid for everything and then he built the altar, offering blood sacrifices for himself and the nation; and the Lord answered him from heaven by fire. Divine fire came down upon those offerings to show God's acceptance and the destroying angel put his sword back in his sheath and the plague was withdrawn from the people. That day, the Holy Spirit replied to the blood that was offered and fire was the voice of His acceptance. Let us now look at the subject of fire –Divine fire.

The God who answers by Fire

In the Old Testament, fire and blood went together so that the sacrifice could ascend to God as a pleasing, soothing aroma. Burnt offerings that had come through blood and fire soothed His Holy Spirit because there's only so much sin that the Lord can tolerate before He has to act in righteous judgment. In Elijah's time, the sins of the people of God had reached 'boiling point' and the whole nation hung in the balances. God wasn't going to allow them to hold two opinions anymore as to who they would love and serve.

They had forgotten the God who had rescued them from the hand of Pharaoh and who had delivered them from slavery in Egypt. They had also forgotten that their God was a jealous God in the sense that He would not tolerate their unfaithfulness to Him and willfully break the covenant that they had once agreed to. It was the Lord then that brought things to a head, challenging them through the words of His prophet Elijah when he said to them all, *"The God who answers by fire, He is God."* By the end of that day, the people would be left with no doubts as to who was the Lord.

1Kings 18:38–39

Then the fire of the Lord fell and consumed the burnt sacrifice, and the wood and the stones and the dust, and it licked up the water that was in the trench. Now when all the people saw it, they fell on their faces; and they said, "The Lord, He is God! The Lord, He is God!"

The fire came and the purging of the people began, beginning with the prophets of Baal. The Greek word for fire is 'pur' from which we get our word 'pure.' Fire brings forth both heat and light and when these things are concentrated, they *purify* the object at hand. Divine Fire speaks of the Presence of God who Himself dwells in such a blinding light that no man can even approach Him without losing his life! Fire brings a sense of the fear of God which the Bible says 'is clean.' Many of us have come to know God is love but we really don't fully understand that the love with which He loves us is a hot, jealous love which grieves at any unfaithfulness or pollution on our part! He will not share us with 'another' for He is a passionate God and fire is His great characteristic!

When God came down on Mount Sinai, He descended in fire and He gave Moses His fiery Law; written by His own fiery finger! This was after meeting Moses in a fiery, burning bush. The redemption of His people was sealed through the blood of the Passover Lamb and then the laws to govern His people were written in fire – Divine fire! *'Our God is a consuming fire!'*

Now let's take a look at the third sanctifying element of God which is water.

The Water of Purification

In the ministry of God in the Old Testament the priest was instructed to take an unblemished red heifer outside the camp where it would be slaughtered before him and then he would sprinkle some of its blood before the Tabernacle of meeting. Then its carcass was to be burned in front of him after which he would wash his clothes and bathe himself in water. The ashes of the burnt offering would be kept for the purification of the ceremonial water.

Numbers 19:9

'Then a man who is clean shall gather up the ashes of the heifer, and store them outside the camp in a clean place; and they shall be kept for the congregation of the children of Israel for the water of purification; it is for purifying from sin.'

The ashes were collected and used in the ceremonial water of purification which is sometimes known as –the 'water of separation.' These waters were purified by the chemicals in the ashes and they were used for the ritual cleansing of the people. The water would be stored in stone water-pots like the ones Jesus used when He turned water into wine at the wedding feast in Cana of Galilee. Water was used for physical and spiritual washing; preparing both body and soul to meet with God.

All these things, the blood, the fire and the water were for the purifying of the worshipper as he presented himself before the Lord.

These of course are all Old Testament examples, based on an inferior covenant and on lesser promises to what we have now in Christ. However, the old covenant with all its particulars was made as a copy of the original Tabernacle in Heaven which God showed Moses; and He commanded him to make everything the same on earth as He had been shown in Heaven. The Bible tells us that this arrangement was going to prevail until the time of reformation and that reformation came through Jesus Christ, who unlike the priests of the Old Testament, ascended into the Tabernacle in Heaven; not with the blood of 'another', but with His own. Coming before the Father, He produced the evidence of 'a life laid down in death.' And it was there and then where He on the basis of His blood, obtained eternal redemption for us! Hallelujah! What a Savior!

As the writer to the Hebrews says: *"If the blood of bulls and goats and the ashes of a heifer could purify the flesh, how much more shall the blood of Christ cleanse your conscience from dead works, (which is empty religion at best) to serve the Living God?"* Christ our eternal High Priest has put away our sins through the sacrifice of Himself! God 'gave us His blood upon the altar' of the Cross of Calvary to make atonement for our souls.

By His blood, we have remission of our sins.

By His blood, we have received atonement for breaking God's holy laws.

By His blood, we have received forgiveness of sins and through faith in His blood we have received our justification before God.

By His blood we have access to the Father and *through* His blood speaking on our behalf; we have received our

17

new position in God; as people without condemnation; the judgement being passed on to Him and carried away.

(You've probably heard it said that "Christianity is not a religion –it's a relationship with God through Jesus Christ." That of course is true, but to be more correct, 'Christianity is firstly a *position* in God *out* of which comes a relationship with God.' No position – no relationship. God can't be your Father until you are His child. It's not enough to believe in God. It's not enough to believe in Jesus. You must be placed *into* Christ; positioned *in* Him who is God's only Son, and *then* you will be saved; *then* you will be accepted by God as one who has been redeemed.

Washed, Sanctified, Justified

If blood, fire and water were essential parts of the Old Testament sacrificial system, how much more shall they now be a part of our New Testament, born again, child of God experience? The ministry of God in the old covenant was temporal by nature but the ministry of God that is now is eternal in nature. The purging elements of God in the new covenant are all manifestations of the Lord Jesus and His Holy Spirit.

1 Corinthians 6:11

'And such were some of you, but you were washed, but you were sanctified, but you were justified in the name of the Lord Jesus and by the Spirit of our God.'

The Holy Spirit is passionate about what He does. He is totally committed to conforming us all to the image of God's Son and to do His work effectively, He has been given everything He needs to get the job done. He has blood, He has fire and He has water. The Lord Jesus has provided the blood – His own precious blood. The Spirit will bring the fire and the water.

Blood! Fire! Water! God has seen fit to give us these things in far greater dimensions than in the old covenant past. In the old sacrificial system these elements spoke *of* Him whereas today they *are* Him and they all come to us through the anointed preaching and teaching of the Word of God. They come through the preaching of the Gospel which is the 'power of God unto salvation.' The message that saves the soul carries with it the blood, the fire and the water. It is faith in Christ's blood that justifies the sinner and it is the Holy Spirit that makes that sinner into a saint through the sanctifying fire of His Word; washing them clean through the 'washing of the Word.' Baptism in physical water awaits all those who have come to know these things as a reality in their spiritual lives.

The pattern for these things was laid down for us in the old covenant ministry in that it was first blood, then fire and then water. The New Testament speaks of the 'saved' as those who have washed their robes and made them white in the blood of the Lamb. This is the first and most fundamental truth of the Gospel that men must yield to. They must confess that they are sinners and that they are trusting Jesus Christ and His blood to save them. There are many decent people in this world (decent in man's estimation), who conduct themselves better than many Christians sometimes, but they will *not* be saved. They will *not* inherit eternal life, because in this life, they never presented themselves as little children at the Cross. They wouldn't get down low enough to get through the 'small door' which is Jesus Christ and they frustrated His Spirit of Grace. They walked away from the 'door' of eternal life disregarding God's offering of reconciliation through the blood of His Son.

For those of us who have gratefully received what God has given, these elements of salvation become the essential principles by which we live. The Lord promised His disciples and us that He would send the Holy Spirit to us and we do well to remember that when the Holy Spirit came to us on the Day of Pentecost, He arrived with the purging elements of God. He came into the world like a 'rushing mighty wind' causing Peter the Apostle to speak boldly to his countrymen about blood, fire and water.

Acts 2:1-4

'When the Day of Pentecost had fully come, they were all with one accord in one place, and suddenly there came a sound from heaven, as of a rushing mighty wind, and it filled the whole house where they were sitting.

Then there appeared to them divided tongues, as of <u>fire</u>, and one sat upon each of them. And they were all filled with the Holy Spirit and began to speak with other tongues, as the Spirit gave them utterance.'

Acts 2:16-21

'But this is what was spoken by the prophet Joel: And it shall come to pass in the last days, says God, that I will pour out of My Spirit on all flesh; Your sons and your daughters shall prophesy, Your young men shall see visions, Your old men shall dream dreams, and on My menservants and on My maidservants I will pour out My Spirit in those days; and they shall prophesy. I will show wonders in heaven above and signs in the earth beneath: <u>Blood</u> and <u>fire</u> and vapor of smoke. The sun shall be turned into darkness, and the moon into <u>blood</u>, before the coming of the great and awesome day of the Lord. And it shall come to pass that whoever calls on the name of the Lord shall be saved.'

Acts 2:38-39

'Then Peter said to them "Repent, and let every one of you be <u>baptized</u> in the name of Jesus Christ for the remission of sins; and you shall receive the gift of the Holy Spirit, for the promise is to you and to your children, and to all who are afar off, as many as the Lord our God will call."'

These are the elements that characterized the coming of the Holy Spirit into the world and you will notice that after these three elements, which agree in unity with each other; the ministry of Christ flowed. Peter and the rest of the apostles having been baptized with the Holy Spirit and fire did many wonders and signs all within the atmosphere of godly fear! The dispensation of the Holy Spirit began with blood, fire and water and will end with them; first the people as on the day of Pentecost and later, the cosmos. All Christian Ministers should know these things and impart them through the anointing of the Holy Spirit upon them. The path for Ministers to fulfill their ministry and glorify God has been clearly laid down in the Scriptures of Truth. There is a Divine order and it goes like this: Blood; Fire; Water; Calling; Ministry Gift; Anointing; Glory!

Let's take one more look into the Old Testament and observe these things in the life of its chief Minister because he walked the path that all God's Ministers tread to one degree or another. His name was Aaron and he was God's high-priest.

Firstly, he knew the *Blood* of the Passover Lamb that saved his life and rescued him from slavery in Egypt. Secondly, he knew the God of *Fire* in the cloud and on the mountain. Thirdly, he was baptized 'into Moses' in the cloud and in the sea; eating the manna that fell and drinking the *Water* that came from the Rock. Before stepping into ministry, he was washed with *Water* because he had been *Called* by God to serve. Then he was *Equipped* for ministry when Moses put on him the holy robes of priestly office; after which he was *Anointed* with oil of separation. Then he knew God in the *Glory* cloud as He filled the Tabernacle and spoke to him from the mercy-seat.

Here is the point of this chapter. We all want the gifting, the anointing and the glory. We talk about very little else. Our regular church services and especially our conferences are full of these things; what they are; why we should have them; and alas, misguidedly, how to achieve them! But if we are truthful with ourselves, truly anointed ministry that walks in the glory of God to-day is conspicuous by its absence! And the reason for that is that we have conveniently forgotten blood, fire and water.

The Priest of the Altar

We have circumvented the altar experience in our lives because none of us want it. The 'altar' is a tough place. Calvary was a tough place! But He who went to Calvary told us plainly that 'if any man would desire to come after Him, let him also, deny himself, take up his cross and follow Him.' God knows how difficult it is for us to lay down our lives in total obedience and He has provided a great High Priest in Jesus who has experienced the human side of things but He can't change the rules for us. God couldn't change the rules for His Son as He struggled with eternal issues in the Garden of Gethsemane and He can't change the order of things just for us.

So the big problem to-day is that the Church by and large, knows little of the 'altar' where blood, fire and water unite. Consequently little is known about Christ as the Priest of the altar. We have often heard how the 'word of God is sharper than any two-edged sword' but rarely do you hear it preached within its context of the altar and its priest.

Hebrews 4:12-15

'For the word of God is living and powerful, and sharper than any two-edged sword, piercing even to the division of soul and spirit, and of joints and marrow, and is a discerner of the thoughts and intents of the heart.

And there is no creature hidden from His sight, but all things are naked and open to the eyes of Him to whom we must give account.

Seeing then that we have a great High Priest who has passed through the heavens, Jesus the Son of God, let us hold fast our confession.

For we do not have a High Priest who cannot sympathize with our weaknesses, but was in all points tempted as we are, yet without sin.'

This is a picture of the High Priest using his knife to slay, cut open and inspect the sacrifice upon the altar; even exposing the joints and the marrow of the bones. This has now become a spiritual experience that all Ministers must go through to one degree or another because *'All things are naked and open to His eyes. There is no creature that is hidden from His sight.'* There's a certain element of dread that goes along with this because exposure is what we fear the most. But this altar has your name on it –so to speak. And so the Lord, the 'priest of the altar' before you experience His power and glory invites you to lay yourself down on it; surrender yourself to Him and allow Him to bring His sword to bear. This is a very hard thing to do but you must do it, because of Who He is and what He's done for you at Calvary; in that *He* laid down His life for *you*. The Bible describes this willingness on your part as *'your reasonable service.'*

'Present your bodies as a living sacrifice, holy, acceptable to God, which is your reasonable service.'

What the Word of God is saying here is: 'all things considered, this is the least that you can do for Him who died for you.'

And so the Holy Spirit brings a situation into your life where it requires you to be obedient. It requires that you surrender your will and like Jesus in Gethsemane, you must say, "Not my will be done, but Your will be done."

You come to Jesus your Priest, and He will help you do what you need to do. He will give you grace in that moment to ascend that altar and then lie down on it; all the while trusting the hand that holds the knife.

And then He will say to you, "This is going to hurt." Yes, the altar is the place for naked, raw truth – you know, the stuff we spend our lives trying to avoid. But never doubt His love for you, because He too was bruised; He too was smitten by God; He too poured out His soul unto death. And as the knife comes down remember the words of Job. "Though He slay me, yet will I trust Him."

Look again at the hands that hold the knife! Do they not also bear the marks of old wounds? There are holes in both His hands and to add irony to it all, He was wounded by His friends!

Let me just add something else that you may find of some comfort in the altar experience. In the Old Testament, as the altars got bigger, they added a ledge all the way around it for the priest to walk upon. He needed the ledge to able to perform his duties with the sacrifices. This ledge gave him the benefit of being able to see everything upon that altar, but it was for his eyes only. Anyone in the vicinity could see something of the sacrifices as they look upwards, but they couldn't see everything like the priest as he looked down on the sacrifice. From that picture of the priest on the ledge we can understand that it's not in the heart of God to humiliate us. Yes, there is a part of the altar experience that goes public for the Cross of Christ was public, but the Lord remembers how delicate we are and so there are things that remain private between you and your priest! *There are some areas of your life that are for His eyes only! Hallelujah!*

After the blood comes the fire. The Holy Spirit will come into your life and sanctify you through your obedience and then you will be ready for the Master's use, and by that time you will be just where He wants you to be. He will find you on the altar of personal obedience – in ashes. This is the moment when you may think that you've got nothing to give but it's out of the ashes that we rise! When the 'old' has gone, the 'new' can come!

It comes as a shock to many to hear that the Lord is not so much looking for their talents but for their ashes! Ashes tell the Lord that blood has been offered and that fire has burned the impurities. And then one of the most beautiful seasons of your life can begin as healing streams of water *pour* through your life to others. Congratulations, you are now a candidate for the Ministry of the Cross of Christ!

Cloths of Service

The Old Testament Ministers of God, Aaron and his sons, who were the priests, wore special 'cloths of service.' They were dressed in 'holy garments' so that they could stand and offer in the Presence of God, being beautified by them and being enabled through them to perform their sacred duties. These garments were to be worn as holy vestments which would not only help them to serve in the sanctuary but they would at the same time protect them from the holy Presence of God. Their work was holy therefore their garments were to be holy also. The High Priest himself was set above the others and therefore his cloths of service were much more impressive, thereby giving a sense of grandeur to his high office. His garments were made of the best materials and they were given to him for 'glory and for beauty.' It is interesting to note that the prescribed articles for him to wear were seven in all, and nearly all of them were put on him from the top downwards; signifying the heavenly endowment of his ministry. Arrayed in these sacred garments the priests would have been made conscious of the dignity of their ministry and the requirements upon them to live out their personal lives accordingly.

To-day in this New Testament era, we don't need special cloths of service because the High Priesthood is now in one Man, Jesus Christ; and it is He alone who dwells in the Presence of God, interceding for us. The old priesthood of Aaron and his sons was abolished when Jesus appeared in the Presence of God with the sacrifice of His own blood. At once, a new priesthood was inaugurated and the old one became obsolete.

Hebrews 8:12

'For the priesthood being changed, of necessity there is also a change of the law.'

The New Testament is all about a new High Priest bringing in a new covenant arrangement with God and man. The tangible holy things of the old sacrificial system have now found their glorious fulfillment in the invisible, yet just as real, Gospel ministry of the Lord Jesus Christ. The Ministers of Christ no longer need or require special 'cloths of service' because they are the born-again, new creations of God where He is their Father and they are His children. The spiritual economy of God in the New Testament is a 'life in the Holy Spirit' where the Christian is seen as a 'true Jew' not in the outward sense but in the inward matters of the heart; not of the outward letter of the Law as on tablets of stone but on tablets of flesh, written by the Spirit of God Himself. We are no longer just *servants* of God; we are now the *children* of God!

However, we still have 'spiritual' clothing experiences in the ministry of the Holy Spirit. Doesn't the New Testament tell us to 'put on the whole armor of God.'? Doesn't it tell us to 'put off our former way of life; our 'old man' and put on the 'new man' which is Christ.'? So to-day, while we do not wear the *physical* clothes of ministry, we still wear the *spiritual* clothes of ministry because the Holy Spirit in His manifold glory rests upon our lives and service.

1 Peter 4:14

'If you are reproached for the name of Christ, blessed are you, for the Spirit of glory and of God rests upon you. On their part He is blasphemed, but on your part He is glorified.'

The Word of God tells us that *'to everything there is a season; a time for every purpose under heaven.'* From this we can safely deduce that the Holy Spirit can clothe us with Himself for whatever heaven decides is needed at that time. If it is a 'time of war' He can clothe us with an indomitable spirit that will fight for the right until the very end. Conversely, He can dress us in His 'meek and quiet' spirit to reconcile warring parties and bring a time of peace to everyone. The Bible talks about the Lord Himself being 'clad with zeal as a cloak' and in all probability this was the 'spiritual' garment that He wore when He brought chaos to the temple in Jerusalem as the merchants there felt the sting of His whip upon them.

On a lighter note, the Bible talks about the Lord giving us the 'garment of praise' to defeat a spirit of heaviness. Our very salvation experience is also spoken of in clothing terms for the Word of God says that *'He has clothed me with the garments of salvation and He has covered me with the robe of righteousness.'* Clearly, the Holy Spirit is able to clothe us spiritually for any kind of season and for any type of work. This has been the glorious modus operandi of the Holy Spirit's manifestations in people's lives in both Old and New Testaments.

Gideon's spiritual Wardrobe

The principles of the Holy Spirit's 'clothing experiences' can be readily seen in the life of Gideon who when the Holy Spirit encountered him, was standing in anything but the right garments, spiritually speaking. By the time the Lord had finished with him, Gideon would become a completely changed man and his 'cloths of service' would differ greatly. When the Angel of the Lord visited Gideon that day, He found him wearing the clothes of 'national shame.'

Judges 6:1-5

'*Then the children of Israel did evil in the sight of the Lord. So the Lord delivered them into the hand of Midian for seven years, and the hand of Midian prevailed against Israel. Because of the Midianites, the children of Israel made for themselves the dens, the caves and the strongholds which are in the mountains. So it was, whenever Israel had sown, Midianites would come up; also Amalekites and the people of the East would come up against them. Then they would encamp against them and destroy the produce of the earth as far as Gaza, and leave no sustenance for Israel, neither sheep nor ox nor donkey. For they would come up with their livestock and their tents, coming in as numerous as locusts; both they and their camels were without number; and they would enter the land to destroy it. So Israel was greatly impoverished because of the Midianites, and the children of Israel cried out to the Lord.*'

This is the season in which the Lord came to Gideon and as it has been proven many times, the only deliverance from the clothes of 'national shame' is to put on the clothes of 'national repentance.' God sent His prophet to them and a 'spirit of contrition' came into the country after hearing his words. God then found His man Gideon, hiding himself from the enemy because when you are wearing the clothes of fear and shame, you tend to hide yourself. (It's the righteous that are as bold as a lion! It's a good conscience towards God that makes you brave!)

So there was Gideon, clothed in the garments of national shame, gripped by a spirit of fear, hiding himself and his food in the winepress. But the Lord had come to change all that! A path to national restoration had begun!

And the first thing that needed to be restored was the covenant that Israel had broken for there can be no victory over the enemy if they have no peace with God! There must be *acceptance vertically* before there can be *power horizontally!* So before anything else, God must first restore peace between Himself and Israel. It was going to take a sacrifice to do that – as always!

Gideon quickly prepared an offering and presented it to the Angel of the Lord whereupon he was then instructed to lay it all out on the surface of a nearby rock. The heavenly visitor then stretched out his staff and put the end of it on the offering. Fire leaped up out of the rock consuming everything and in the blink of the eye, the Angel was gone!

Judges 6:24

'*So Gideon built an altar there to the Lord, and called it The Lord is Peace.*'

An acceptable *sacrifice* on an acceptable *altar* by an acceptable *man* has always been what God has required. This is a picture of Calvary where God's acceptable Man gave an acceptable offering on an acceptable altar.

It was there in the prophetic shadow of Abraham's sacrifice of Isaac on the mountains of Moriah that peace with God was provided. The altar of the Cross of Christ can certainly be called 'Jehovah Shalom' just like Gideon called his altar many years beforehand.

Family Clothes

From that moment, Gideon was released from his clothes of national shame. He stood there that day as a new man in God! However, there were still some clothes on him that needed removing, and he didn't even realize that they were on him! They had been on him since he was a child. They were the clothes of his father! They were the clothes of his ancestors. Let's call them 'family clothes.' Not everything in your family is bad, but not everything in your family is good!

Gideon's father had clothes of idolatry – spiritual adultery in that his house was a *center* for false gods. Before Gideon can bring deliverance to the nation, he must first take out of his life the bondages of his father's idolatry! A daunting challenge lay ahead for Gideon and to accomplish it he would have to undergo his first 'wardrobe change.'

Gideon must put on the spiritual blood-red coat of suffering for the will of God.

(The apostle Paul described this coat as the 'afflictions of Christ in his body.' Queen Esther wore these 'red garments' when she put her own life on the line with the king, saying, *"If I perish, I perish!"* Jesus of Nazareth wore this red robe both spiritually and physically as He stood broken and bleeding before Pontius Pilate at His trial.)

The Lord instructed Gideon to tear down his father's altar to Baal and to cut down the wooden idol next to it. He was afraid to do it in the day time so he and ten other men did all the damage under the cover of darkness. When morning came the men of the city were very angry at what they saw and what had obviously happened during that night.

Judges 6:29

'So they said to one another, "Who has done this thing?" And when they had enquired and asked, they said, "Gideon the son of Joash has done this thing."'

Gideon narrowly escaped death that morning but he had done what he needed to do. The idolatrous headship of his father needed to be broken off him, for the Holy Spirit required a free man to do the work of a free Spirit.

And so it is the same for us, in that there can be no full release of authority in our ministries while we're still wearing the ancestral clothes. While it has to be said that God is *for* family unity, sometimes, in order to set us free, He has to bring a crisis of obedience into our lives where we have to be *seen* to cut some family ties. It can be incredibly difficult to do but sometimes it has to be done! When Jesus first began His ministry, His own dear mother tried to pull the 'strings' on Him at the wedding feast when they ran out of wine. The Lord had to cut that 'apron string' right there and then! I'm sure it wasn't easy for Him, but the anointing on His head was from His Heavenly Father and not His earthly mother!

We must all examine our parents and grandparents in the light of God's Word and thank God for everything they got right and try and change everything they got wrong. Then we must give *our* children the permission to do the same with *us* when they're older! None of us are perfect are we? If we do these things in a 'spirit of grace' we will discover that as the light of God increases throughout the generations, the spiritual fruit that comes from our families increases in the kingdom of God.

Gideon now stood ready for the battle that was looming ahead. God had changed the season to a 'time of war' and a new spiritual clothing experience was coming his way! He was to be clothed in the heavenly blue garments of the Holy Spirit's power. The enemies of Israel came into the land again in vast numbers to do what they had done many times before but the spiritual atmosphere had now changed in the nation and so the Spirit of God came upon Gideon.

Judges 6:34

The literal translation is this: 'The Spirit of the Lord *clothed* Himself upon Gideon.' The Holy Spirit wrapped Himself around the body of Gideon, and *then* he blew a trumpet for war, and the local men gathered to him. (This is a picture of the Day of Pentecost, when the Holy Spirit came upon the disciples and they blew a spiritual trumpet, for out of their mouths came loud heavenly sounds and the tongues of men and angels were heard in Jerusalem; and the multitude was gathered to them.)

Clothes of Commission

These spiritual, heavenly blue clothes of the Holy Spirit are the 'clothes of commission.' A commission is 'an authorization to perform certain duties and to take on certain powers.' Gideon's experience that day was akin to the apostles on the Day of Pentecost when as Jesus promised, they were endued with power from on high. *"You shall receive power when the Holy Spirit has come upon you"* Jesus said.

These powers are the spiritual equipment to do the work of the Lord. In the New Testament, they are known as 'the gifts of the Holy Spirit' and they are the new covenant 'cloths of service' with which to serve the Lord. We wear them in the sanctuary to serve the people of God and we wear them to fight the battles of the Lord in the world outside. *These then are the holy garments that New Testament Ministers wear.* They are invisible to the human eye but in the spiritual world everything living in that dimension knows if a Minister has them on or not!

Elijah wore these clothes when he called down fire from Heaven.

Elisha wore these clothes when he struck the River Jordan, saying "Where is the Lord God of Elijah?" The disciples of the Lord wore these clothes when they were sent out in pairs to go and exercise their new authority over all the power of the enemy: and it seems that the demons recognized the 'cloths of service' that they were all wearing because they immediately obeyed the disciples commands when they were addressed.

Clothes of a Clown

Gideon was ready for the fight, but wisdom had a surprise waiting for him.

'For the race is not to the swift, nor the battle to the strong.' For Gideon to win this battle and for God to get the glory, he was going to have to wear the 'clothes of a clown.' He was going to have to prove that *'the foolishness of God is wiser than men and the weakness of God is stronger than men.'*

God took Gideon down from thirty-two thousand men to only three hundred men! He must come to know by experience that awkward truth in God that *'when he is weak, then he is strong.'* Gideon must now be willing to become a fool for Christ's sake. Noah wore these clown's clothes when he was building that boat! Naaman the general of the Syrian army wore these clothes when he had to dip seven times in the River Jordan to receive his healing. *These* 'cloths of service' are the most difficult to wear but they are extremely effective in the work of the Lord. These spiritual clothes are for the mature Ministers of Christ who have to their surprise, discovered that sometimes in God, to go forward one must first go into reverse. It's a painful procedure because you look like you're failing and your decisions are difficult to explain and much of what you're doing doesn't make much sense to you either!

In the service of the 'wars of the Lord' there is such a thing as a tactical retreat and so all movements that the Holy Spirit inspires must be carefully considered. What is a catapult and what does it do? Is it not an instrument of war that takes the missile back first, and then when the tension is cut, the missile is thrown forward at great speed? This is how God wins wars in your life. He reverses and reduces you first; helps you overcome your fear of failure; and then he catapults you forward!

The slaughter of the Midianites was so great that day, that it became a proverb in Israel. For any subsequent huge military victory by the people of God, they would say, *"As it was in the day of Midian!"* If you want your life to make a huge impact for God, you have to be prepared to look a bit foolish and wear 'cloths of service' that make you look small before they make you look great.

Gifts and Graces

All these 'clothing experiences' are manifestation of the varied gifts and graces of the Holy Spirit. He is the life and power behind our ministries and now that Christ has been glorified as a Man in heaven, He is now able to come to us as the children of God and give us a taste of the powers of the world to come! In the age to come, it will not be placed under the hand of angels; it will be placed under the hand of man and so it is God's will that we experience that future authority now through the agency of the Holy Spirit. Signs, wonders and miracles are to be done through us as the Holy Spirit wills. Added to them are the ministry gifts of people whom the Spirit of God has singularly blessed to serve in various offices of His administration. To some, He gives the 'cloths' of an apostle; to some a prophet; to some an evangelist; to some a pastor and to some a teacher. These then are the 'cloths of service' that New Testament Ministers wear because all the physical, tangible ones of the Old Testament have been made obsolete. Christ has given us not only a better arrangement with God; He's given us the 'promise of the Father' which is His Holy Spirit.

Truly, the 'cloths of service' that we have been given in Jesus are of a much higher order than those that Aaron and his sons wore in the Tabernacle. God has clothed us with the 'Spirit of Glory and of God' and He has made us able Ministers of the new covenant blessings in Christ Jesus.

Both the old sacrificial system and the new covenant arrangement in Christ's blood were and are holy things. The beautiful yet sacred garments were put on the priests so that they could be in the Presence of God and not die whilst performing their ministry. As has been previously stated, their work was holy therefore their garments must be holy. Moreover, their 'cloths of service' were linked to their very lives.

Numbers 20:25-28

"'Take Aaron and Eleazar his son, and bring them up to Mount Hor; and strip Aaron of his garments and put them on Eleazar his son; for Aaron shall be gathered to his people and die there." So Moses did just as the Lord commanded, and they went up to Mount Hor in the sight of all the congregation.

Moses stripped Aaron of his garments and put them on Eleazar his son; and Auron died there on the top of the mountain. Then Moses and Eleazar came down from the mountain.'

This solemn moment forever stands as a principle of a Minister's calling in that His life and testimony are not over until his last breath. Ministry service can change in many ways over a life time and it can even diminish in the closing years but there is no real retirement in God's service. As long as the Minister is alive, he is a witness and a testimony to others. When the work is truly over, his 'cloths of service' are left on this side of the 'River' and he walks out into the light of glory with the words of the Lord ringing in his ears, *"Well done, good and faithful servant. You were faithful over a few things, I will make you ruler over many things. Enter into the joy of your Lord."*

New, heavenly, eternal clothes will be given to the Minister as he is welcomed on the other side by those who've gone before him. He will be given a white robe in which he will both live and serve the Lord who bought him – forever!

The Anointing Oil

The anointing oil is an element of Divine ministry because it is a symbol of the Holy Spirit. The very name 'Messiah' means 'Anointed One.' Those who are called to minister in His Name will receive from Him an anointing of the Holy Spirit of one degree or another, according to the gift of Christ in their lives. It is the anointing of the Holy Spirit that sets us apart from the profane and establishes us in our sacred office. The pouring of oil upon the head of the Minister is the outward sign that the invisible Spirit of glory and of God has now come to rest upon that individual. This of course is clearly seen in the Old Testament Ministers but it's still a spiritual reality in those who have been called to preach the Gospel of Christ. Let's study this subject by looking at the Divine protocols found in the Old Testament and then observe its outworking in a New Testament setting.

The concept and even practice of making someone or something sacred has been in the minds of men since their primal existence. We know for sure that the patriarch Jacob knew of its significance because after he had dreamt of the ladder going up to heaven, he took the stone upon which he had laid his head and set it up on top of a pillar of stones, pouring oil upon it. As the oil ran down from the top of the pillar, he dedicated that place to the Lord and renamed it. The place where the oil was flowing down from the top of the pillar, he called 'Beth-el' which is the 'House of God.' Thereafter, the anointing oil being a symbol of the Lord would be forever linked to the consecration and the ministry of the House of God - be it Tabernacle, Temple or Body of Christ. This emphasis of the oil flowing down from the head of the House of God manifests itself again with the Ministers of the Tabernacle as they are anointed with holy oil on *their* heads.

Anointed Priests
Exodus 29:4-9

'And Aaron and his sons you shall bring to the door of the tabernacle of meeting, and you shall wash them with water. Then you shall take the garments, put the tunic on Aaron, and the robe of the ephod, the ephod, and the breastplate, and gird him with the intricately woven band of the ephod.

You shall put the turban on his head, and put the holy crown on the turban. And you shall take the anointing oil, pour it on his head, and anoint him. Then you shall bring his sons and put tunics on them with sashes, Aaron and his sons, and put the hats on them. The priesthood shall be theirs for a perpetual statute. So you shall consecrate Aaron and his sons.'

The anointing oil would be poured over Aaron's head in copious amounts for the psalmist indicates that it was sufficient to run down his beard and even to the hem of his garments. This fulfills the pattern of the 'pillar of Jacob' and it was in effect a form of baptism in that the oil of the Holy Spirit flowed from the top to the bottom; touching the whole man. He was at that point viewed as holy; as consecrated to God and to the service of God in His House.

Not only were the *Ministers* of the sanctuary anointed with oil, so was the *House* of God and everything in it. In Aaron's ministry, the Tabernacle and *all* its sacred furniture were anointed with the holy oil.

Exodus 40: 9-11

'And you shall take the anointing oil, and anoint the tabernacle and all that is in it; and you shall hallow it and all its utensils, and it shall be holy.

You shall anoint the altar of the burnt offering and all its utensils, and consecrate the altar. The altar shall be most holy.

And you shall anoint the laver and its base, and consecrate it.'

The holy oil was put on all the things pertaining to the House of God and it was the head of the High Priest that bore the chief aspect of it all. What is important to observe about the dedication of the ministry through the anointing oil is that wherever the oil was, there was the Holy Spirit. This was God's ministry and God's oil. He gave the ingredients and the composition to Moses with the solemn command that it was to be reserved for sacred purposes only. No one was allowed to make anything like it for themselves and so copies of it were strictly forbidden. It was to be used for holy purposes both in the sanctuary for the priests, and for prophets and kings in the world. And so it was that any life that was set apart for Divine office or Divine purpose knew something of the anointing of God because it was the Holy Spirit upon their heads that was enabling them. This was the reason why they were so successful in their endeavors and why they enjoyed such unusual protection.

Anointed Kings

The first king of Israel, Saul, was anointed with oil as was David and his son Solomon. In Saul's case, the prophet Samuel came to him and taking a flask of oil, he poured its contents on his head and declared in that moment how the Lord had 'anointed him to be king and commander over His inheritance.'

Young David was also discovered through the revelation of the Holy Spirit to the prophet Samuel and he was anointed with oil in the midst of his older brothers. In each case, after the oil had been applied, the Spirit of the Lord came upon each man. There was a direct correlation between the oil and the Spirit. All that was needed to maintain that experience was a holy life but sadly, Saul became very rebellious and he disobeyed God in many things. He brought God to the point where He regretted putting him into office and that is why the Lord rejected him and found David to take his place. King Saul lost his anointing! He remained in charge of the nation but he was reigning on his own; for God had left him and where the Spirit of the Lord had once been, there now came an evil spirit from the Lord to torment him. The head that had once rested in the peace that the Lord had given was now full of tormenting thoughts which brought destruction to him and his family. In the end, God removed him and in the course of the never-ending battles with the Philistines, he died through the wounds of war. Like many Ministers before and after him, Saul forgot that he was carrying 'hot coals of fire' in that sacred duties are best performed by holy men.

Anointed Authorities

In Saul and David, we see the perpetual struggles between freshly anointed ministry and diminishing once-anointed ministry. Finding a working harmony between the two is almost impossible because one is hanging on to his position while the other is destined to take it! There is a saying in the world that says, "He who has the gold, rules." In the Divine administrations of God, I think that it can be said that "He who has the oil will eventually rule." I say 'eventually' because in the economy of God, it's not just the man's *life* that is anointed; it's the man's *office* that is under the Spirit of God. The office itself carries God's authority and therefore it has a residue of the Holy Spirit upon its function. This is a very important truth to understand because in a generation that exalts the 'spirit of man' in that folks nowadays would like to think that leadership is only influence, it can come as a bit of a shock! Most people to-day will openly say that they could only follow somebody they respect and while God understands those sentiments, nevertheless, with God, office is office and authority is authority; whether we admire the person or not! In the Ministry of God, leadership is not only influence, it is position; it is title and it is office.

David himself knew this to be true because when he was given an opportunity to take Saul's life and with one stroke, remove the bane of his life, he wouldn't do it. Even though the Lord's Spirit had for the most part, left Saul, David still viewed him as the 'Lord's anointed' because a residue of the Spirit remained upon him at least while he was still the king.

1 Samuel 24:5-7

'Now it happened afterward that David's heart troubled him because he had cut Saul's robe. And he said to his men, "The Lord

forbid that I should do this thing to my master, the Lord's anointed, to stretch out my hand against him, seeing he is the anointed of the Lord."

So David restrained his servants with these words, and did not allow them to rise against Saul. And Saul got up from the cave and went on his way.'

Although their personal relationship had completely broken down, David still viewed Saul as his master and because of that headship of Saul over his life; David wouldn't touch him nor let any of his servants harm him. David understood that as long as Saul was still king, that he was still to be regarded as the Lord's anointed by reason of office.

David would be tested again on this very matter when once again; he was given an opportunity to remove Saul from his life once and for all.

1 Samuel 26: 8-11

'Then Abishai said to David, "God has delivered your enemy into your hand this day, Now therefore, please, let me strike him at once with the spear, right to the earth; and I will not have to strike him a second time!"

But David said to Abishai, "Do not destroy him; for who can stretch out his hand against the Lord's anointed, and be guiltless?"

David said furthermore, "As the Lord lives, the Lord shall strike him, or his day shall come to die, or he shall go out to battle and perish. The Lord forbid that I should stretch out my hand against the Lord's anointed."'

David knew that if he killed Saul that he would have walked into a conflict with the Holy Spirit of God and that would have been bad for him both personally and publicly. The guilt he would have brought upon himself would have been great for *"Who can stretch out his hand against the Lord's anointed and be innocent?"* It's questionable if God in those days would have accepted a sacrifice in atonement for a sin like that.

The difficulty for us is found in the dichotomy between a man and his office; where the man is no longer reflecting the sacredness of his office and yet he remains in position. There is a clear example of this in the New Testament when it comes to the high priest in Jesus' day; the one named Caiaphas. At the closing of our Lord's life here on earth, Caiaphas was officiating as high priest in the nation. He was anything but the right man for the job but the anointing oil was still on him because of the position he held and the title he had.

John 11:47-53

'Then the chief priests and the Pharisees gathered a council and said, "What shall we do? For this Man works many signs. If we let him alone like this, everyone will believe in Him, and the Romans will come and take away both our place and nation."

And one of them, Caiaphas, being high priest that year, said to them "You know nothing at all, nor do you consider that it is expedient for us that one man should die for the people, and not that the whole nation should perish."

Now this he did not say on his own authority; but being high priest that year he prophesied that Jesus would die for the nation, and not for that nation only, but also that He would gather together in one the children of God who were scattered abroad.

Then from that day on, they plotted to put Him to death.'

Caiaphas was a man who had a heart that was far away from God's and yet he was able to prophesy in the Holy Spirit by reason of the office in which he stood. Because he was the high priest of Israel that year, there was a residue of the Holy Spirit on him through the anointing oil and so not only did he understand more than his contemporaries; he was also able to bring the final adjudication concerning Jesus at the council. Like King Saul, though Caiaphas was far away from the Lord, he was still able to function at that council as the 'Lord's anointed.' The Lord Jesus Himself recognized this reality and it's interesting to observe that when question after question was being hurled at Him, He remained silent until Caiaphas as high priest demanded that He speak. Caiaphas said to Jesus, *"I adjure You by the Living God: Tell us if You are the Christ, the Son of God!"* Jesus replied, *"It is as you said."*

Even the apostle Paul at his trial was quick to retract some accusatory statements that he had made to a Jewish official there when he discovered that the man was the high priest.

Touching the anointing of God in a bad way is tantamount to touching the Holy Spirit and His life and power. Who can disrespect that which has been made sacred to God and expect no consequences?

Holy Matrimony

This spiritual reality also pertains to marriage where couples have been joined in holy matrimony before God. When God is sought to bless a union, He anoints that marriage with the graces of His Spirit and so a residue of the Spirit rests upon it.

When in the Old Testament, the priests and the people had fallen away from God, they began to cast off the restraints of the past and many of the Ministers were cheating on their wives and some were dissolving their marriages. God had to remind them that by harming their marriages and by committing sexual sin with those already married, that they were touching the Holy Spirit who had anointed them as one.

Malachi 2:13-16

'And this is the second thing you do; You cover the altar of the Lord with tears, with weeping and crying; So He does not regard the offering anymore, nor receive it with goodwill from your hands.

Yet you say, "For what reason?" Because the Lord has been witness between you and the wife of your youth, with whom you have dealt treacherously; yet she is your companion and your wife by covenant.

But did He not make them one, having a remnant of the Spirit? And why one? He seeks godly offspring. Therefore take heed to your spirit and let none deal treacherously with the wife of his youth.

For the Lord God of Israel says that He hates divorce, for it covers one's garment with violence" says the Lord of hosts. "Therefore take heed to your spirit, that you do not deal treacherously."'

In a generation of loose morals, it has become much more socially acceptable for people to commit adultery, referring to such behavior as 'having an affair.' The Lord knows that some are sincerely hurting in their marriages and he knows that there is a lot of private pain being experienced 'behind closed doors.' To such as those, His heart is grieving. What the Lord is saying here to the priests of the past and to the Ministers of to-day, is that to seek a sexual relationship with an already married woman would bring them into conflict not just with men but also with God! Adultery touches that which the Holy Spirit has anointed with His grace and who can stretch out his hand in that arena and not grieve the Holy Spirit?

'That which God has joined together, let no man put asunder'!

There was a king called Abimelech who encountered this reality when he unwittingly took Abraham's wife Sarah to be his own. To be fair to him, Abraham had not told him the truth and because of that God showed Abimelech and his family mercy. God spoke to him in a dream one night saying, *"Restore the man's wife; for he is a prophet and he will pray for you and you shall live."* This he did promptly and his household was healed.

Well said David when he recalled the faithfulness of God to his ancestors recounting what the Lord had said to foreign kings: *"Do not touch My anointed ones and do My prophets no harm."*

The anointing oil then speaks of the consecration of both people and things to God for His glory and for His use. The pouring of the oil on their heads is a picture of the actual Holy Spirit of God coming upon them to separate them from the world for sacred duties. The oil is reflective of a measure of the Holy Spirit who guards their lives and ministry office; enabling them to perform all the functions necessary. And the wonderful thing about the anointing oil of God is that the Holy Spirit is ever fresh and the hope of the Psalmist and each one of us is that *'the Lord will anoint us with fresh oil.'*

May we all be faithful to Him who is our head –the Lord Jesus Christ whom God anointed with power and who went about doing good and healing all who were oppressed by the devil, for God was with Him! He is the Messiah – the 'Anointed One.'

For Jesus Sake

If the previous chapters have been describing what we do and how we do it, then this chapter will answer *why* we do what we do. This chapter's contents touch the very reasons why we do the things we do and so while simple in its substance, these forthcoming paragraphs are not without their challenge; for anything that reveals our motives will always present a moment for us to 'consider our ways.' This chapter therefore will at the very least, serve as a reminder to us to not forget the main thing. And what is the main thing? The main thing is a person. His name is Jesus!

'For Jesus' sake.' Think about that prayerful comment for a moment. It's not a phrase you hear much nowadays. You might hear the phrase 'In Jesus' Name' - which is fine, but I remember that when I was a child, I would often hear my grandfather say at the end of his prayers – "For Jesus' sake, Amen." I heard other people of that generation also end their prayers with the same words. Even when they were saying the 'grace' over their food, they would end that prayer with the words "For Jesus' sake, Amen."

So, the question is: "Why has that particular phrase largely disappeared from our vocabulary?" Is it perhaps that we have lost sight of the main thing? Is it perhaps that, over the years we've made this thing more about us than about Him?

Let me remind us all that the Cross is the central event of all time and that the Man on the Cross is the central figure of all time. God has placed Him there at the center of it all and He is without rival!

Let's have a look at what the Scriptures tell us about what God has done and will yet do, for His Son, Jesus. Let's listen again to the apostle Paul as he explains to us what the ministry is all about.

2 Corinthians 4:5-7

'For we do not preach ourselves, but Christ Jesus the Lord, and ourselves your bondservants for Jesus' sake. For it is the God who commanded light to shine out of darkness, who has shone in our hearts to give the light of the knowledge of the glory of God in the face of Jesus Christ.

But we have this treasure in earthen vessels, that the excellence of the power may be of God and not of us.'

Wow! 'We do not preach ourselves –but Christ Jesus the Lord!' Brothers and sisters, the ministry starts and finishes right there! Paul is saying that we are not self-promoters, seeking elevation for ourselves. No, we preach and we hail Christ Jesus the Lord and we have made ourselves into servants of the church, for Jesus' sake! We've done this so that He can be glorified in us and in His church, which is His Body.

'The treasure and the excellence of the power is of God and *not* of us!'

Paul goes on to say that as Christ's Ministers, we've signed up for a life of difficulty as well as life of great joy, and that we must embrace the 'afflictions of the Gospel' for Jesus' sake! Many trials come our way and they can at times bring a kind of death experience to *us*, but it ends with Christ's life shining out of us for the benefit of *others*.

Paul further explains the reasons for these tough personal experiences by revealing some of the things that had happened to him.

2 Corinthians 12:7-10

'And lest I should be exalted above measure by the abundance of the revelations, a thorn in the flesh was given to me, a messenger of Satan to buffet me, lest I be exalted above measure.

Concerning this thing I pleaded with the Lord three times that it might depart from me. And He said to me, "My grace is sufficient for you, for My strength is made perfect in weakness."

Therefore most gladly I will rather boast in my infirmities, that the power of Christ may rest upon me. Therefore I take pleasure in infirmities, in reproaches, in needs, in persecutions, in distresses for Christ's sake. For when I am weak, then I am strong.'

Many people have tried to identify Paul's 'thorn in the flesh' -that 'messenger of Satan' with pin-point accuracy, but it still remains in a shroud of mystery if the truth be told. However, Paul goes on to say what effects took place in his life and ministry after he had learned to embrace it. For Christ's sake and the Gospel, Paul received an *'afflicting spirit'* which brought into his life, infirmities, reproaches, needs, persecutions, and distresses. All of these things took a toll on him, but he learned the secret of the Lord in that when he was weak, then he was strong. He accepted all those negative things in his life for Jesus' sake; so that the power of Christ could rest upon him and that the Lord's interests in the world could be accomplished.

He suffered for His Name's sake. He suffered the loss of everything for Jesus's sake and for His Body's sake which is His church; whom Christ purchased with His own blood. And that is the key to understanding this whole matter –the saints of God; the Body of Christ; otherwise known as the 'family of God.'

All Things are for Him

From before the world began, the intention of God was to have a family made in His own image and that this Body of chosen people would be taken from the family of man and given as a Bride to His one and only, beloved Son.

That is why the New Testament tells us that God has forgiven us for Christ's sake!

God loves us deeply and He wants to free us from our sins and give us eternal life, but the main reason that God has chosen to forgive us *in* Jesus is so that Jesus can have an inheritance *in* us! The Cross of Jesus' death was all about reconciling the world to God so that through redemption of the 'purchased possession' the Lord could have a people; a Bride of His own! What a double truth! The Church has an inheritance in Christ and Christ has an inheritance in us! The Man Christ Jesus has made this possible! If nobody could be saved, from where would the Lord get a people for Himself who are spiritually 'of His flesh and of His bones'? Paul prayed for the Ephesians that *'they would know what is the hope of His calling and what are the riches of the glory of His inheritance in the saints.'*

The saints of all ages are the elect of God. They were chosen in Christ from the foundation of the world and they are the ones whom God has saved and sanctified for Jesus's sake!

Even a cursory look at the Scriptures will tell us that the story of this world doesn't end well. This age will end in destruction for the wicked, but amazingly, for those whom God has saved, it ends in a wedding!

"Blessed are those who have been invited to the marriage supper of the Lamb!" says the final book of the Bible.

Revelation 19:7

'Let us be glad and rejoice and give Him glory, for the marriage of the Lamb has come, and His wife has made herself ready.'

This will be the time that the Lord has been waiting for. In that moment, He will be joined to His bride in holy matrimony and the Church, the saints of God, will be His forever! *We will be His and He will be ours; and we will all be God's. Hallelujah!*

This heavenly marriage is what redemptive history has been all about. It has not just been about human civilization trundling its way through eons without point or purpose. No, James tells us, that God the Heavenly Farmer has been waiting all this time for 'the precious fruit of the earth' and when that time is up; when the fields are fully ripe, He will send His angels into the world to reap. *"Thrust in your sickle now and reap, for the harvest of the earth is ripe!"* He will say.

The last trumpet will sound and God will send His Son Jesus to come in the clouds of the sky, ready to resurrect His saints to eternal life. He will descend to answer the prayer of the Holy Spirit and the Bride, who will be saying together "Come, Lord Jesus!" As the old hymn used to say, "Come, Lord Jesus, take Thy waiting people home!" *'And so we shall ever be with the Lord.'*

Oh! The joy that is waiting for Jesus! Oh! How satisfied the Father will be to see His Son so happy and joyful with us, His inheritance.

Let us all remember that everything God does is with His Son in mind. Everything the Son did and still does is with His Father in mind. And God the Father has given His Holy Spirit to His Son, so that the Son might pour Him out upon us to glorify Him. The Holy Spirit has been sent from Heaven for our sakes, so that we might be saved and so that we might serve. The Holy Spirit enables us to do these things because He glorifies Jesus and everything the Holy Spirit does on earth is with the Son of God in mind. (That is why He's so grieved when Ministers stand up and promote themselves, and do not preach 'Jesus Christ is Lord' with a perfect heart.)

We've talked about the past and we've talked about the future, but where is the Lord's inheritance to be found today. Well, many of the saints of God are already home with Him in Heaven, but where are the rest? They are here on the earth made up of those that are saved and those who are yet to be saved. The redemption rights are now fully in the Lord's hands and there's nothing on earth that isn't rightfully is. He alone has *'crushed the serpent's head'* and *'through death, He destroyed him who had the power of death, that is, the devil.'* God has promised Him the *'nations for His inheritance and the ends of the earth for His possession.'*

His Inheritance

The nations of the world are His inheritance and so within the mystery of God's will, the Holy Spirit works to rescue from the condemnation that's in the world, all the saints of God in every generation. Our job is to go into the entire world and preach the wonderful Gospel of God, for it is the only message that can save a soul from eternal death. Just as you would find veins of gold buried in the hills and mountains and just as you would find pearls in the depths of the seas, so there are hidden treasures in the nations of the world. They look like very ordinary people, and that's because they are! In fact, most of them are probably poor but God has an inheritance in them for His Son! God has chosen many of the poor in this world to be rich in faith; that they might be saved and become heirs of the Kingdom of God.

Throughout the centuries, the world has stood aghast upon seeing Christian missionaries leave the comforts of 'hearth and home' to sail away into the great unknown. With tears of love being shed by themselves and their loved ones; they've walked up many a gang plank to board the ships that will sail to far off lands; taking them to heathen peoples' who've never heard the Gospel of Jesus Christ. Some leave their shores knowing that the missionaries who went before them were murdered by the natives upon arrival! Some have gone to climates where tropical diseases have claimed so many because the average life span of a jungle missionary in those days was approximately five years! Others have been even willing to commit themselves to leper colonies; greatly endangering their own health in the hope that they might win some of them to Jesus!

What then was the underlying motivation for all those wonderful personal sacrifices? It was simply yet profoundly this: that Christ had an inheritance in the heathen and they all believed the Scriptures when it said *"How shall they believe in Him of whom they have not heard? And how shall they hear without a preacher?"*

They did all those things and they ran all those risks so that the lost ones could hear the only message that could save them. In so doing, they were offering their lives in service, not for themselves but for Jesus' sake. The Lord Jesus has an inheritance in every tribe, tongue and nation and we owe it to Him to take His light into the darkness, and thereby extend His kingdom among men. So, we do what we do for whose sake? 'For Jesus' sake.' May God help us never to forget it!

The Fear that is Good

The Bible tells us that there is a 'season for everything' -which means that there is a time and a context in which even fear is a *good* thing. And yes, there is a time and a context in which fear is a *bad* thing but in this chapter I want us to see when fear is not just a good thing –it's a *God*-thing!

Let us first observe this godly fear in our spiritual father Abraham whom we know was a 'Friend of God' and yet at the same time had a healthy 'fear of God.' It is interesting to note that when Abraham was just about to sacrifice his son Isaac that the Angel of the Lord stopped those proceedings with these words: *"Do not lay your hand on the lad, or do anything to him; for now I know that you fear God, since you have not withheld your son, your only son, from Me."* The Angel of the Lord didn't say, *"Now I know that you love God"* or *"Now I know that you have faith in God"* but *"Now I know that you FEAR God."* Our father Abraham passed that test on account of His fear of God. I am sure that he loved God to, but his obedience came as a result of His godly fear.

Any plain reading of the Scriptures will tell us that the main 'love-language' of God if you will, is obedience. Abraham's son Isaac was singularly blessed in his life because his father had *obeyed* God's voice and kept His charge, His commandments, His statutes and His laws. Jesus said it clearly to His disciples and to us: *"If you love Me, keep My commandments –just as I have kept My Father's commandments and I abide in His love."*

What was the motivation for the Lord's obedience? We know that the love between Him and His Father was profound but that wasn't all. Because He was a Son, He gave His Father His obedience through the fear of Him in His life. The prophet Isaiah foretold that the anointing that would be upon the Messiah would be manifold: that on the 'Anointed One' there would be a Spirit of wisdom and understanding; a Spirit of counsel and might; and a Spirit of knowledge and of the fear of the Lord. In fact, Isaiah goes on to say, that *'His delight will be in the fear of the Lord!'* So let me put this respectfully: While Jesus walked this earth as a man, He lived and performed His ministry according to these two principles – the *love* of God and the *fear* of God. He dwelt in His Father's love and He made sure He was obedient to His commandments. He rejoiced in the liberty that His Father's love gave Him and He loved the air of discipline that His Father's fear gave Him. He delighted in both!

In God the Father's heart, you will find that love and fear dwell perfectly together. In fact, they provide the perfect blend as they are both wrapped up in God's light. *So I think it's safe to say that if the love of God can save us; then the fear of God will keep us!*

We've always been taught that 'perfect love casts *out* fear' and that is true for it casts out the fear that is *bad*. God has not given us that kind of spirit because it's not God's will that we should be tormented but there is a fear that is *good* and it's called the 'Fear of the Lord.' As was previously noted, Abraham loved God but he passed the test because he *feared* God.

The Holy Spirit of Fear

This Holy Spirit of Fear was passed on to his son Isaac and his son Jacob knew the Lord by *this* name –the Fear of Isaac! Later, his descendants would come out of Egypt because God had redeemed them through the blood of the Passover Lamb and then He sent the Angel of His Presence to lead them into the Promised Land. At that time, God said this about the Angel of His Presence: *"Beware of Him: obey His voice and do not provoke Him for He will not pardon your transgressions; for My Name is in Him."* God loved Jacob and his descendants and they became the 'apple of His eye' as He led them through the wilderness; carrying them on His 'wings.' However, God saw fit to add to that relationship of love the awesome fear of His Presence at Mount Sinai.

'Now all the people witnessed the thunderings, the lightning flashes, the sound of the trumpet, and the mountain smoking; and when the people saw it, they trembled and stood afar off.

Then they said to Moses, "You speak with us, and we will hear; but let not God speak with us, lest we die."

And Moses said to the people, "Do not fear; for God has come to test you, and that His fear may be before you, so that you may not sin."'

As you can see then, the people of God have *always* had these two aspects of the Lord in their lives. To have *only one* of these will at the very least mean an imbalance in your spiritual life. If all you know is the 'love of God' you may become slack in some things and when His 'rod of correction' comes into your life, your relationship with God can momentarily break down because you neither knew nor expected His judgements.

Alternatively, if all you know about God is how He ought to be feared, you will never know what it's like to have His love surround you. You may *believe* in Almighty God but you will never *know* Him as your Abba Father –which is the endearing term of 'Daddy.' You'll spend your whole Christian life with a feeling of distance – a feeling He doesn't ever want you to have!

The Bible uses many words to describe fear and all the definitions tend to go like this: 'Fear is reverence; respect; regard; awe; and even terror.'

The apostle Paul when writing to the Corinthians about the Judgement Seat of Christ (at which every believer will make an appearance) appealed to them to live a life pleasing to Christ in light of His terror!

Where is My reverence?

In the very last book of the Old Testament, it reveals the lamentable heart condition of the people of God at that time and especially of those involved in the ministry. Over the years, the people by degrees had lost the fear of the Lord. He had become less and less relevant to them in their daily lives and the priests, the Ministers of the Sanctuary were just going through the motions; not caring about what God might think. The nation had lost respect for the ministry and the priests themselves were shamefully offering to God their scraps. So the Lord came to them through the prophetic word of Malachi and He brought His case to them.

He first told them again of how much He loved them; how He had taken care of them as Jacob's descendants while at the same time He had destroyed his brother Esau's heritage. Then He brought His case to the 'gates of their hearts.'

Malachi 1:6

"A son honors his father, and a servant his master. If then I am the Father, where is My honor? And if I am a Master, where is My reverence? says the Lord of Hosts to you priests who despise My name."

We have a common saying now and it goes something like this: *"If anyone wants my respect, they're going to have to earn it!"*

We can all admit that there is a certain element of truth in that statement. However there is a flaw in it because it is saying that *"I will decide who gets my respect regardless of their position in my life."* But there are some people who warrant your respect just because of *who* they are. *'Honor your father and your mother'* says the Word of God. You are to honor your parents as much as you can because it is the right thing to do; it is the noble thing to do and it is the godly thing to do.

God Himself is our Father and He says to all His children to-day: *"If I am a Father, where is My honor? If I am a Master, a Ruler, then where is my reverence; where is my fear?"*

v14(b) *"For I am a great King, says the Lord of Hosts and My Name is to be feared among the nations."*

In both the Old and the New Testaments we are told the same thing. *'Fear God and keep His commandments.' 'Fear God and honor the king'* –honor the president; honor the senate and the congress; honor the governors and *all* those in authority. Why? Because all authority comes from God and His throne and while we are living on the earth, we must honor authority whenever we can and wherever we encounter it. (There *are* exceptions when situations arise and we find that we must obey God rather than men; but those times are rare and *if* we must disobey, we must do it in the right spirit. There can be no foul language or shaking of the fist for those whose lives are truly 'under God.')

Honor to whom Honor

'Render therefore to all their due: taxes to whom taxes are due, customs to whom customs, fear to whom fear, honor to whom honor.'

There are many other Scriptures that tell us to obey the ordinances of man for the Lord's sake and for our conscience's sake. Honor everybody. As a Christian and most certainly as a Minister, give respect and value to everyone you meet. *"Servants, employees: give your masters or your employers fear and respect —even the bull-headed ones! Wives, be submissive to your husbands. Show them respect —even the bull-headed ones!"*

As the 'spirit of man' becomes increasingly rebellious, it cannot help but resist authority and authority figures more and more. Law and order are put to severe tests as people see fit to tear down the fabric of society. Institutions long held sacred are undermined with each successive generation and morals continue their inevitable slide. The value of a human life erodes, not being regarded like it used to be. All of these things are largely due to society losing its fear of God.

To-day, the atheism of the past has caught up with us to give a mind-set where God is at best seen as benevolent yet irrelevant. However *we're* largely to blame for that because for generations now, we've only celebrated His love and not delighted in His fear! Consequently, there are vast numbers of Christians who don't believe that God will judge us. The truth is that He is judging us *and* the world *all* the time! He's still on the throne, weighing the hearts of men and judging their deeds. His commandments haven't changed and His word is still there to be obeyed and the troubles that we are facing now are because we have forgotten that.

King David forgot that. There was a time in his young life when David had the love of God and the fear of God working sublimely together. Those were the days when he walked very carefully before God and when opportunities came his way to finish off King Saul and solve all his immediate problems, he was afraid to lay his hand against his master the king –the Lord's anointed authority.

Later, David became King in Saul's place. He took the throne and Saul's wives and it was good for many years but 'time and power' are rarely a good mixture for men. When people hold power for a long time, they tend to change, and David began to lose the fear that was good. It was only a matter of time until he would commit the great sin of his life –the adultery with Bathsheba and the murder of her husband.

2 Samuel 12:7-10

'Thus says the Lord God of Israel: "I anointed you king over Israel, and I delivered you from the hand of Saul. I gave you your master's house and your master's wives into your keeping, and gave you the house of Judah. And if that had been too little, I also would have given you much more!

Why have you despised the commandment of the Lord, to do evil in His sight? You have killed Uriah the Hittite with the sword; you have taken his wife to be your wife, and have killed him with the sword of the people of Ammon.

Now therefore, the sword shall never depart from your house, because you have despised Me, and have taken the wife of Uriah the Hittite to be your wife."'

The question the Lord had for David was this: "Why have you despised the commandment of the Lord, to do evil in His sight?" Did David love the Lord? Yes, he did. David would shower the Lord with his affections through his music and through his poetry. Did David fear the Lord? Obviously not – at least not at that time in his life! No one who fears the Lord will despise the Lord's commandment! I think it's fair to say that not only did David *not* fear the Lord but at that time *he loved himself more* than God! He would have known that what he was doing was very wrong but he chose to do it anyway. The fact that he went ahead and did the things he did shows a hardening of the heart and a dulling of the conscience. It shows us that if *we* lose our fear of God *we* may even end up losing *our* love for God! Brothers and sisters in Christ, we need them both! There have been many Ministers who got themselves into big troubles all because they lost or never knew the fear that is good! It has been said 'that the state of the nation rests on the state of the pulpit.' If the 'fear that is good' is missing from the pulpit how can we expect it to be in the congregation? And if it's missing in the Church, how can we expect to see it in society? If *Christians* are rebellious to authority, where will the world be on these matters?

Respect and Revere

As the Ministers of God, we have a responsibility to walk ourselves in the fear of the Lord and then inculcate its precepts into the congregations that we serve. In a time where even the lofty wooden pulpit has had to make way for the Perspex lectern; we have an extra burden upon us to ensure that at least in God's House, the Lord is held in honor and in reverent fear.

The apostle Peter affirms this when He told us that '*the Father, without partiality, judges each one according to his works and that we should conduct ourselves throughout the time of our stay down here –in fear!*' The Word of God teaches us to respect and revere God and all the authorities that He has set up –both visible and invisible! The Lord told His people to be careful how they talked about the magisterial powers over them.

"Do not revile God or the ruler of your people" was His admonition. What does 'revile' mean? It means to rant and rave; to talk violently; to slander and injure with malicious disrespect. The New Testament tells us that even the archangel Michael didn't revile Satan when he disputed with him about the body of Moses. He did not dare bring a railing accusation against Satan in his higher authority, but said to the Devil, *"The Lord rebuke you."*

The Greek word that describes a 'railing accusation' is 'blasphemia' –

'*O be careful little mouth what you say!' 'Do not rebuke an older man but exhort him as a father'* said the apostle Paul to Timothy; yet how many Christians to-day have taken the liberty to rebuke their pastors openly? Where did they get the justification to do that? They got it from the world. They received that attitude from the spirit of this world which says "You tell him like it is. You stand up in front of the congregation and tell him a few home truths! After all, who does he think he is?" In a generation of rebellion people don't fully understand the nature of authority and therefore they are unaware of what they are really 'touching.' The apostle Paul wrote to the Romans, *"Whoever resists the authority resists the ordinance of God, and those who resist will bring judgement on themselves."* Many Christians have taken their cue from the world and allowed the over familiarization of people and things to cloud their judgement and they run into trouble with God, because they have forgotten the sanctity of the ministry. When the people of God lose 'the fear that is good' they eventually lose respect for God's Ministers; for God's House and for God Himself!

As Ministers of Christ we must not fail to give the people of God the 'whole counsel of God' and that includes His fear. If *we* don't fear God and His judgments; if *we* don't regard His commandments and respect His authorities, what chance does the one in the pew have of understanding these things? How long will it be before both Church and society come apart at the seams?

Yes, there is a 'fear that is good.' There is a godly fear that saves from sin and harm. Embrace it! Be like Jesus and delight in it! Be a good Minister. Be a good Christian. Be a good citizen. Be a good employee, *'obeying your employers in all things, not with eyeservice as men-pleasers, but in sincerity of heart, fearing God.'* Be a good employer *'for there is a Master in Heaven over you!'* Be a good patient; be a good driver; be punctual. All of these things are born out of respect, which comes from a spirit of reverence, which is rooted in the 'fear of the Lord.'

The 'Fear of God' is the first domino to fall in the moral slide of a nation that once knew better and it begins with us the Ministers when we fail to live it and refuse to preach it!

Don't be like many who only drink the cordial of His love –to the point of intoxication where they think that He would never bring His rod of reproof into their lives. Deception in this area now runs so deep that there are many Christians to-day who actually think that even if they sinned in a very bad way, that God would make an exception for them! We dare not allow ourselves to be deceived and the antidote to that false notion is to acknowledge God's requirement of holiness in our lives. So let your heart be warmed by the cordial of His love and also drink the purgative drink of His fear just as the Psalmist declared –*'the fear of the Lord is clean, enduring forever.'*

The word of God will *make* you clean and the fear of God will *keep* you clean! Embrace then, the 'fear that is good.' Be like Jesus and delight in it!

Finally, the Bible tells us in the Book of Hebrews that one of the reasons that God heard the prayers of Jesus was because of His godly fear! He was the Son of God and yet He was known in heaven for His godly fear. If this pertained to the life of Jesus, how much more to us?

Nobility in the Ministry

'Nobility' has been used as a social term to describe the upper classes; those who by high birth or station have constituted the ruling class. They were known as 'the aristocracy' which literally means 'the best rule.' In practical terms it was 'government by a privileged minority' most of whom had inherited their wealth and social position. Any member of this ruling class was regarded as a 'nobleman.'

However, the origin of the word 'noble' speaks of elevation –not by birth, but through self-education; because it comes from two Latin words which means 'to get to know' or 'to find out.' As King Solomon once said: *'It is the glory of God to conceal a matter, but the glory of kings to search out a matter.'* This 'seeking to know' – this 'seeking to understand' is what has produced the characteristics of the truly noble; for noble implies loftiness of character; elevation in thoughts and in principles, along with a constant adhering to them. Other words such as honorable, worthy, integrity, magnanimous –all well describe the *spirit of nobility*. The opposite of noble is ignoble, which means to be base; to be vulgar or common.

While we know that human nature is dark, nevertheless we were created in the image of God and there have been many people down through the centuries that have become noble in heart and mind. They have made themselves into men and women of 'high principle' and through self-education of the Scriptures; they have served God in much higher ways than they would have normally lived their lives. The Lord's first disciples, the fishermen were like this. One only has to read their epistles to appreciate that their writings are the work of noble men! What about John Bunyan who was as poor as the proverbial church mouse? He was known as the tinker of Bedford –but read his works, like 'Pilgrim's Progress' and the 'Holy War' and you will find that they are the works of a spiritual genius! Jesus of Nazareth, the son of a carpenter had the leaders of His day amazed at his teaching and His understanding. *"How does this Man know letters, having never studied?"* they said of Him. So, there have been *individuals* that despite their backgrounds, have displayed great nobility of character; but what is also fascinating is that the *grace of nobility* can be found in whole *families*! Sometimes you can find in certain families, a 'thread of honor' that can be traced back for generations.

One of the reasons God blessed Abraham was based on the fact that God knew that Abraham would teach his children and his descendants the ways of the Lord. And so it has been with other families who have faithfully passed on the spirit of true nobility onto their children and their grandchildren. Like a rich man's legacy, the 'spirit of nobility' has then been a spiritual inheritance that has traveled down the line of their descendants!

As Ministers of Christ, we must never lose the 'common touch' but having the Lord and the Scriptures in our lives should produce a higher level of living. By God's grace we have been given a higher level of understanding and we walk through this life with the Living God! All of these things should prove to be of great benefit to our families and to those we serve. Let us take a look at a Scriptural example of nobility running through a family line.

The Rechabites
Jeremiah 35:1-10

'The word which came to Jeremiah from the Lord in the days of Jehoiakim the son of Josiah, the king of Judah, saying, "Go to the house of the Rechabites, speak to them, and bring them into the house of the Lord, into one of the chambers, and give them wine to drink."

Then I took Jaazaniah the son of Jeremiah, the son of Habazziniah, his brothers and all his sons, and the whole house of the Rechabites, and I brought them into the house of the Lord into the chamber of the sons of Hanan the son of Igdaliah, a man of God, which was by the chambers of the princes, above the chamber of Maaseiah the son of Shalum, the keeper of the door.

Then I set before the sons of the house of the Rechabites bowls full of wine, and cups; and I said to them "Drink wine." But they said, "We will drink no wine, for Jonadab the son of Rechab, our father, commanded us, saying, 'You shall drink no wine, you nor your sons forever. You shall not build a house, sow seed, plant a vineyard, nor have any of these; but all your days you shall dwell in tents, that you may live many days in the land where you are sojourners.'

"Thus we have obeyed the voice of Jonadab the son of Rechab, our father, in all that he charged us, to drink no wine all our days, we, our wives, our sons, or our daughters, nor build ourselves houses to dwell in; nor do we have vineyard, field or seed. But we have dwelt in tents and have obeyed and done according to all that Jonadab our father commanded us.

There was a 'spirit of nobility' in the family of the Rechabites that God saw and respected. He knew that they were principled men who wouldn't compromise their father's and their grandfather's commands. And how that pleased Him! Here they were, a small band of people living in Jerusalem that were unlike His own people in that they were a family of noble degree. Their ancestors had once lived very secure in a fortified city, but they and everyone else had been scattered by the Assyrian army when the northern kingdom of Israel fell into their hands. Thereafter, their fore-father's commands were for them to be always sober and to take up the nomadic life of living in tents to ensure the survival of their family line. This they did until the day that King Nebuchadnezzar's army invaded the Holy Land and it was then decided by them all to flee to Jerusalem for protection.

Jeremiah 35:12-19

'Then came the word of the Lord to Jeremiah, saying, "Thus says the Lord of hosts, the God of Israel: 'Go and tell the men of Judah and the inhabitants of Jerusalem, "Will you not receive instruction to obey My words?" says the Lord. "The words of Jonadab the son of Rechab, which he commanded his sons, not to drink wine are performed; for to this day they drink none, and obey their father's commandment. But although I have spoken to you, rising early and speaking, you did not obey Me.

I have also sent to you all My servants the prophets, rising up early and sending them, saying, 'Turn now everyone from his evil way, amend your doings, and do not go after other gods to serve them; then you will dwell in the land which I have given you and your fathers.' But you have not inclined your ear, nor obeyed Me.

"Surely the sons of Jonadab the son of Rechab have performed the commandment of their father, which he commanded them, but this people has not obeyed Me."'

You can sense the deep frustration that was in the heart of God over the willfulness and rebellion of His own people. As a Father to them all, He had lovingly commanded them to amend their ways and obey His voice but they wouldn't even listen never mind perform. Exasperated, He confirmed that all the doom that had been previously pronounced upon them and the city would now come to pass because He had spoken and they hadn't listened. He had called out to them but they didn't answer Him. However, the Lord wasn't going to allow truly noble people to be destroyed in the war that was coming. God looked kindly on the Rechabite family because they were faithful to their father's commandments, even when they were given an opportunity to break their promises. *"We will drink no wine"* they said.

The outcome of this holy exercise was for the Rechabites to receive a promise from the Almighty; that they would *not* perish in the soon-coming war, but that they would always have a living representative before God.

Jeremiah 35:18-19

'And Jeremiah said to the house of the Rechabites, "Thus says the Lord of hosts, the God of Israel: 'Because you have obeyed the commandment of Jonadab your father, and kept all his precepts and done according to all that he commanded you, 'therefore thus says the Lord of hosts, the God of Israel: "Jonadab the son of Rechab shall not lack a man to stand before Me forever."'

The very thing they had feared was gone forever. They had feared extinction but God proved their nobility of character and promised to take care of them.

What a family! Where did that integrity come from? It came from Jonadab, the son of Rechab. Where did Rechab come from? Where did he receive those noble principles of honoring *his* father? Well, let us be 'kingly' in our hearts and like Solomon, let us *search out the matter*. Let us be noble ourselves and *seek to find out* through the Scriptures where such loftiness of character came from. From where did such regard towards their forefathers commands come from? There are a few things of note in their family line and so I'd like to go back up the line a step at a time and maybe we'll understand where such principled people came from.

The Scribes at Jabez

Everybody knows about Jabez; how that God granted his request and enlarged his borders; but people tend to forget that the Scriptures record that 'Jabez was *more honorable* than his brethren.' Jabez possessed a degree of nobility that his brothers didn't have and God blessed him for that. It is possible that his borders increased to the point where a whole city was built and named after him – the city called Jabez. We don't know for sure, but we do know that honorable men just like Jabez lived in this city. They were men who studied the Scriptures. They were men of noble mind who wanted to find things out and search deep matters concerning the Living God. And guess what? They weren't even Jews! They were the ancestors of the Rechabites. The Bible tells us that they were scribes.

1 Chronicles 2: 55

'And the families of the scribes who dwelt at Jabez were the Tirathites, the Shimeathites and the Suchathites. These were the Kenites who came from Hammath, the father of the house of Rechab.'

'These were the *Kenites* who came from *Hammath*, the father of the house of *Rechab*.' This particular chapter in Chronicles is about Judah and his descendants and last but not least, added onto the list is this Kenite family of scribes who are somehow a part of them. These were noble men living alongside a noble tribe in Israel; even serving them as scribes in the Word of God and probably in other legal matters. These people weren't just in the land; they were *scribes* within the community. They were men of high thought and social elevation among the Children of Israel! How did this happen? Well, we know when they got their visas! These folks got their 'visas' to enter the Promised Land the same time that the tribe of Judah got theirs! When it came time to fight for the Promised Land, this family, along with the tribes of Judah and Simeon were among the first to 'stand up and be counted' for war.

Judges 1:16

'The children of the Kenite, Moses' father-in-law went up from Jericho with the children of Judah into the Wilderness of Judah, which lies in the South near Arad; and they went and dwelt among the people.'

These people came from the in-laws of Moses. Moses' wife Zipporah had six sisters and no doubt there were some of them still living along with their husbands and children. They were the descendants of a great man called Jethro who although a Kenite was of such spiritual stature that he became the priest of Midian.

Exodus 18:8–12

'And Jethro said, "Blessed be the Lord, who has delivered you out of the hand of the Egyptians and out of the hand of Pharaoh, and who has delivered the people from under the hand of the Egyptians.

Now I know that the Lord is greater than all, the gods; for in the very thing in which they behaved proudly, He was above them."

Then Jethro, Moses' father-in-law offered a burnt offering and other sacrifices to God. And Aaron came with all the elders of Israel to eat bread with Moses' father-in-law before God.'

Jethro was a great man –the priest of a nation and a role model in some ways for Aaron before he himself was inaugurated as the high priest of Israel. Upon hearing the confirming testimony of Moses concerning what God had done for them in Egypt, Jethro rejoiced and blessed the Lord for showing Himself greater than all the gods! He then offered sacrifices unto the Lord, and Aaron came with all the elders of Israel to eat and fellowship with him and with Moses. So, this great man Jethro was a Kenite and he was the priest of Midian. Midian was a son of Abraham! All of Abraham's sons were blessed; even Ishmael whom he had to send away. God promised Abraham that he would bless him because he *was* his son. Midian was also blessed and he had five sons who then grew in population and lived near the smaller Kenite families. Jethro was not born into the Midianite aristocracy but there was obviously something special about him and somewhere along the line, his inherent nobility stood out and spoke for itself; and they made him a priest among them, even though he was a Kenite.

The Grace of Nobility

Looking at the Scriptures, I am persuaded that true nobility is a *grace* from God; and that whilst it can be the sole property of an individual, I believe it can also be a family trait throughout many generations. I like what Paul said to Timothy when he spoke about the genuine faith that was in him; and how it had dwelt first in his grandmother Lois and then in his own mother Eunice. The Bible gives us sufficient proof to show that God has put graces upon families; a nobility of sorts, where legacies of faithfulness; of obedience; of purity; of richness of thought, speech and spiritual understanding can be found. We can be grateful to God that He has seen fit to honor the spiritual legacy of a 'noble man' by extending his qualities through his descendants long after he has gone! Such families are blessed by God and like the Rechabites, they enjoy heaven's esteem.

Contrary to them are those who *choose* to be base; who *willingly* go through life without due care and attention; mocking at the self-restrictions of the noble; and then one day, they wake up in Hell! 'Wisdom' cried out in the streets to them: she raised up her voice in the open public squares, but they chose not to listen to her; and her warnings went unheeded. They refused to stop their lives and seek out the matter; to know and find out what God and life were loudly saying to them. They were *ignoble* and as they were happy in their ignorance they were eventually caught like fish in the net!

2 Peter 2:10-13

'Those who walk according to the flesh in the lust of uncleanness and despise authority are presumptuous, self-willed. They are not afraid to speak evil of dignitaries, whereas angels, who are greater in power and might, do not bring a reviling accusation against them before the Lord, But these, like natural brute beasts made to be caught and destroyed, speak evil of the things they do not understand, and will utterly perish in their own corruption and

will receive the wages of unrighteousness, as those who count it pleasure to carouse in the daytime.'

The apostle Paul described the men that he fought with at Ephesus as 'beasts' and the mob that came for him at Thessalonica as men of the baser sort. In things concerning the kingdom of God, ignorance is not bliss! When the hearts and minds of men are locked into their baser instincts, their behavior becomes degrading and shameful. They live dishonorable lives and even rejoice in their ignorance; becoming unaware of how disgraceful they appear. Thankfully, the apostle Paul met a higher minded set of folks when he and Silas visited Berea.

The Bereans
Acts 17:10-11

'Then the brethren immediately sent Paul and Silas away by night to Berea. When they arrived, they went into the synagogue of the Jews.

These were more noble than those in Thessalonica, in that they received the word with all readiness, and searched the Scriptures daily to find out whether these things were so.'

Because the Jews in Berea were more noble than the Jews at Thessalonica, the Gospel of the Lord Jesus Christ found an attentive audience. They were fair-minded people who were willing to hear a matter and then proceed to do research on it. They had a willingness to put themselves about to find out whether what they had heard was scripturally true or not! The Jews in Thessalonica were filled with envy towards Paul and so they fought against him without too much thought at all! Such then is the mentality of the mob. They arrive on the scene with sticks in their hands because they haven't thought in their heads. They are just like the people at Ephesus who filled the city amphitheater in anger, but they didn't really know why they were there. But look what happened to those who were noble in the synagogue in Berea.

Acts 17:12

'Therefore, many of them believed, and also not a few of the Greeks, prominent women as well as men.'

When people can be persuaded to have an open mind towards the Scriptures, it can more easily lead them to faith. This fair-minded approach requires a sense of nobility from them because all pre-conceived notions have to be put to one side. Unfortunately, most people have their minds made up on spiritual things even if they don't understand them but the one who has a noble heart is 'not far from the kingdom.'

To those who have been called to preach the Gospel of the kingdom should there not be a trace of true nobility found in them? Should not those who teach the very words of God live by higher principles than most? Should not the Ministers of Christ live honorably among the people they serve? Should there not be found in them a loftiness of character and a magnanimity of soul that allows them to walk tall in a base world?

My father told me of an incident that he remembered from his youth when he and some of his friends were playing in some derelict houses. In those buildings there were many pigeons, all of which were of the common sort. And then, all of a sudden, another pigeon flew into the old house and it stood out from the rest. The way it looked; the way it walked; and the way it held its head made it stand out from the rest. It was in fact a racing pigeon that had momentarily lost its way home. It was a pigeon just like the others but it had a grace upon it that set it apart from the rest. There was a sense of nobility in that bird that wasn't found in the others and it walked among them like a king. Should not the Ministers of Christ possess higher qualities than most through the grace that has been given to them? Should they not walk as princes among men? If Jesus Christ is both Lord and King, should not His servants reflect their Sovereign? Are we not His ambassadors?

Lessons from a rogue Minister

Judges 17:1-13

'Now there was a man from the mountains of Ephraim, whose name was Micah. And he said to his mother, "The eleven hundred shekels of silver that were taken from you, and on which you put a curse, even saying in my ears —here is the silver with me; I took it." And his mother said, "May you be blessed by the Lord, my son!"

So when he had returned the eleven hundred shekels of silver to his mother, his mother said, "I had wholly dedicated the silver from my hand to the Lord for my son, to make a carved image and a molded image; now therefore, I will return it to you." Thus he returned the silver to his mother. Then his mother took two hundred shekels of silver and gave them to the silversmith, and he made it into a carved image and a molded image; and they were in the house of Micah.

The man Micah had a shrine and made an ephod and household idols; and he consecrated one of his sons, who became his priest.

In those days there was no king in Israel; everyone did what was right in his own eyes. Now there was a young man from Bethlehem in Judah, of the family of Judah; he was a Levite, and he was staying there. The man departed from the city of Bethlehem in Judah to stay *wherever he could find a place. Then he came to the mountains of Ephraim, to the house of Micah, as he journeyed.*

And Micah said to him, "Where do you come from?" So he said to him, "I am a Levite from Bethlehem in Judah, and I am on my way to find a place to stay." Micah said to him, "Dwell with me, and be a father and a priest to me, and I will give you ten shekels of silver per year, a suit of clothes, and your sustenance." So the Levite went in.

Then the Levite was content to dwell with the man; and the young man became like one of his sons to him. So Micah consecrated the Levite, and the young man became his priest, and lived in the house of Micah. Then Micah said, "Now I know that the Lord will be good to me, since I have a Levite as priest!"

Soon after the death of Joshua and the elders of Israel, the people of God having no king or supreme commander, fell into idolatry and all the dark things that accompany it. This is always the case when everybody just does what they want, when they want. We find this scenario vividly portrayed for us in the Book of Judges as the nation goes through the sad cycles of doing well when God gives them a leader and then doing badly when they've been left to their own devices. When Israel had a judge from God, they obeyed and they were blessed; but as soon as that judge died, they collapsed morally and then militarily. It remains as a lesson for all nations; that the people who do what's right in their own eyes will soon end up doing evil in the sight of the Lord. And one of the first casualties of a backslidden nation is its neglect of the House of God and of its Ministers. God warned His people not to forget the Levites that were dwelling among them because they had no inheritance in the land; and they were to be supported by the other tribes of Israel. These then were the prevailing conditions in the nation of Israel at this time.

Micah

Our story begins with a man called Micah and his mother. His mother had saved a lot of money and it came to eleven hundred shekels of silver. It had been in her mind – so she said; that upon her death, her son Micah would inherit it. Micah was a fully grown man having a family of his own. In fact, he had one son of priestly age, and it appears that Micah for one reason or another had wanted his mother's money right there and then. So he took it. He knew where she kept it and he stole it. He robbed his *own* mother! I have a feeling that the mother suspected her son to be the thief because she began to call down a curse on the 'robber' in *his* hearing! As she was screaming out curses, I'm sure that his ears were burning.

Can you see what the love of money can do? It destroys relationships. It caused Micah to rob his own mother and it caused his mother to willingly forget all her natural affections for her son and glibly curse him -if he had indeed taken the money. (It has been said that when good people lose money, it drives them to their prayers; but when bad people lose money, it drives them to their curses.) I think that this woman's silver was a god to her long before she made it into graven images.

Micah had second thoughts about it all. He probably thought to himself *"It's better to wait for the money and have my mother's blessing than to keep it and have my mother's curse."* So it was 'own up time' and he confessed to his mother what he had done. She immediately withdrew her previous malediction and pronounced a blessing from the Lord upon him. He gave back to her the money he stole and they were reconciled, but the 'deceitfulness of riches' remained in the fabric of their characters. She originally said that she had

81

dedicated *all* the silver to the Lord after which it was to be then given to her son to make a couple of silver images or idols. But when it came down to it, when it came to the point of handing the silver over; the original eleven hundred pieces became two hundred pieces. (Funny how some people's math can work out when it concerns their money! I have found that people who love money will always promise much but deliver little. It's like they have to 'cough it up' – like an exorcism of sorts. Covetous people have a tendency to do math differently to others.)

She gave the two hundred shekels of silver to the silversmith and the silversmith made two images; two silver idols for Micah. Then Micah made a part of his house into a little chapel, a house of God, so the Septuagint said; a house of error, so said the ancient Chaldean manuscripts. It was a dark mixture of all those things and it became a shrine for him and his family; making one of his sons wear the ephod of a priest. Meanwhile, the true house of God, with its true priests and the true oracles of the priest's Urim and Thummin were located at Shiloh. And it was at Shiloh where the 'gathering of the people' should be and *not* at some private shrine of a local, wealthy, influential man!

So, while Micah was supposedly honoring God with these silver images, he was in fact breaking the commandments of God through Moses. He was in fact, bringing evil spirits into his house and into the land of Israel. Not only did he have silver idols in his home, he then went ahead and consecrated his own son (probably his eldest son) to be a priest! Only the sons of Aaron were set apart by God to function as priests *and* in the designated place of the Tabernacle with the altar of burnt offering. Here we see Micah trying to get all the personal benefits of religion without coming under the authority of God's true tabernacle and God's true representatives. This is the kind of thing that happens when people do what is right in their own eyes and they conveniently forget all the proscriptions of God.

There was no king, judge, or magistrate to convince Micah of his error, either to restrain him or punish him. Such then were the times when these events took place.

The Young Levite

Into this lamentable situation comes a young man from Bethlehem. He is a Levite and he is looking for a place to live and make a living through the performance of his spiritual duties. He came to the mountains of Ephraim and to the house of Micah, where money had already been an issue. Stepping into that atmosphere there would begin an issue in his own life concerning his own ministerial ambitions and the questions that would hang over his life would be these: "What's the most important thing –the ministry or the money?" Additionally, "What is better –praise from God or praise from men?"

This young minister had been living in Bethlehem but it seems that he had been moving about the region quite a lot before he stayed there. Bethlehem was not a Levite town and things didn't seem to be working out well for him there so he once again left where he was and he began rambling around the countryside. (This 'rambling around' is a chief characteristic of a Minister that's lost his spiritual way. He's got a sense of the call of God upon His life but he lacks the direction of God.) So, he leaves Bethlehem for 'wherever' and looks for full time ministry somewhere else. He travels into the hill country of Ephraim and he arrives at the house of Micah, and Micah can't believe his good fortune! The young man told him that he was a Levite and that he was looking for a place to stay. Micah immediately invited him to stay with him and his family and then he went straight to the deal. He told the young Levite that he would make him to be a father and a priest to the whole family; and that he would pay him ten shekels of silver a year, along with new clothes and lodging.

I don't know how Micah's son –the one who had been made as a priest to the family felt about this new development, but as we have already seen, a man who loves money loves the deal. Actually, for the man who already has money, the deal is what he lives for. It's all about the *next* deal and such an attitude can easily cancel out all previous promises and understandings; even those made to your own children! The love of money destroys relationships! Notice also, that Micah made this deal without any 'due diligence' on behalf of his family. There were no enquiries as to whether the young man was a Levite or not; or if he had a good testimony in the places where he had once lived. No search was made to prove the young minister's integrity and Micah's haste to get the deal done could have put his family at risk. What if this young man wasn't what he seemed? What if he had been an ill-tempered young man with a violent past? What if he had been in trouble due to lust problems? So many questions surrounded this stranger, but Micah went by his instincts and took him in. Fortunately, Micah's immediate perceptions of the young man were on target and the young man fit so well within the family that he became like a son to Micah.

This shows us that this young Levite was in most people's eyes, a decent young man. However, there can always be serious flaws in the nicest of people and it's only a 'lack of opportunity' that keeps the lid on their proclivities. He will, like most Ministers of God be tested not by trial, but by something more challenging –by opportunity! The 'door' to his ambitions opened up that day when Micah offered him the job to become the family priest. He accepted the post and so Micah consecrated him to be his priest and to officiate at his home-built shrine.

Micah was so happy. In *his* mind, he thought that he had just sealed the deal with God Himself! To have a Levite to be his own personal, family priest, guaranteed the blessings of God upon his life – or so he thought.

Now, if this young Levite had any real conscience towards God, he would not have allowed this situation to develop, for he would have known that only Aaron's sons were called by God to be priests to the nation. Also, to serve the Lord through one man's silver images was in direct opposition to what God had commanded through Moses. This entire situation was just plain wrong! And as a Levite, he must have known it. The young minister had a choice to make: the ministry or the money? What was it to be? God's calling or Micah's deal? God's service or Micah's silver?

Well, it looks like he came under the spell of Micah's house where just as it had been with Micah and his mother, money and its power became the priority. He chose payment of services over purity of ministry –and do you know what? The wages weren't *that* good! (I think that if God has called you to ministry, then don't run away from it or find a lifestyle outside of it. I think that a man who forsakes his ministry calling for a secular job makes the worst trade in the world, because even if you make a good living in this life, you will be the poorer in the life to come –and that one lasts forever!)

Well, as is usual in life, there came a day when everything changed. As they say, "Change is here to stay." Unfortunately for Micah, change would come to his door once more, only this time he would not gain from it. He would in fact lose badly.

The Men of Dan

Enter now into the story the men from the tribe of Dan. This tribe would eventually find and take their inheritance in the northern part of the Promised Land but at the time of this story, they were living in some of the towns allotted to the tribe of Judah. They had agreed among themselves that it was time to seek their own land inheritance and so they sent five out of their ranks to go and search for it.

Judges 18:2-7

'*So the children of Dan sent five men of their family from their territory, men of valor from Zorah and Eshtaol, to spy out the land and search it. They said to them, "Go, search the land." So they went to the mountains of Ephraim, to the house of Micah, and lodged there.*

While they were at the house of Micah, they recognized the voice of the young Levite. They turned aside and said to him, "Who brought you here? What are you doing in this place? What do you have here?"

And he said to them, "Thus and so Micah did for me. He has hired me, and I have become his priest." So they said to him, "Please inquire of God, that we may know whether the journey on which we go will be prosperous."

And the priest said to them, "Go in peace. The presence of the Lord be with you on your way." So the five men departed and went to Laish.'

One day, the search party of the tribe of Dan came to Micah's house. They met him and the family, and when they heard the voice of the young Levite, they recognized him. It seems that this young Levite had been living in *their* cities before he had found his way to Bethlehem. (His track record suggests that we have a bit of a rogue minister here, a bit of a 'caballero' -a man on the move. In the world, they are called 'fortune-seekers' or 'opportunists' and it seems that these characteristics of worldly ambition were in this young man.)

The Danites said to him, "Who brought *you* here? What are *you* doing in this place? What have *you* got going on here?"

He told them the story and how he had been hired by Micah to be his priest. When they saw him functioning as a priest, they asked him to inquire of the Lord for *them* to see if *their* journey to find *their* inheritance would be successful. And so they left, but within a short space of time they were back; but this time they returned with six hundred men who stood at gate of the property of Micah. The five men who had been there before greeted the young Levite priest and as he went to the gate of Micah's property to meet the six hundred men and their families, the five men entered the shrine chapel and stole all the religious artifacts that were in there. They came walking up the road with the silver images, the ephod and all the household idols. The young priest protested to them, but they just told him to be quiet. They could see that this situation could be awkward for him so they made him a deal that was hard for him to refuse. *"Do you want to be a priest to the household of one man or do you want to be a priest to a tribe and family in Israel?"*

"Deal or no Deal?"

He had to decide in a moment, but it wasn't too difficult for him. When he heard the deal, he was glad in his heart. He took hold of the ephod and the household idols and quickly took his place among them. It was quite easy really. After all, he was used to moving out – he'd been on the move for years. Opportunity called again –and off he went, as was his custom.

Micah got to hear what had happened and he and his neighbors caught up with the Danites and complained bitterly to them about what they had done to him. *"You have taken away my gods which I made, and the priest, and you have gone away!"* The Danites told Micah to be quiet or else he could pay with his life and his family's too! And when he saw that they were too strong for him, he went back home minus a priest and with the loss of all his silver icons. This time, *he* was robbed! It wasn't right of course, but sometimes, 'might overcome right.'

The Danites conquered the main city of the area where their inheritance lay for it had been granted to them from the Lord through Moses and Joshua. But the 'seed of the serpent' was hidden in the bushes of their victory and the idols of Micah became the idols of the tribe of Dan. The virus of idolatry had been inserted into the tribe and over the years the infection spread. The descendants of Dan, the son of Jacob, had false gods and a false priesthood. (It's interesting to note that in the Book of the Revelation, it says that twelve thousand men are set apart for God from each of the tribes of Israel – all the tribes apart from Dan!)

Judges 18:30-31

'Then the children of Dan set up for themselves the carved image; and Jonathan the son of Gershom, the son of Manasseh, and his sons were priests to the tribe of Dan until the day of the captivity of the land.

So they set up for themselves Micah's carved image which he made, all the time that the house of God was in Shiloh.'

The idols of Micah were set up by the Danites themselves and then here comes the real shocker! The Scriptures reveal who this young Levite was. His name was Jonathan, and it seems that he was the grandson of Moses! Was this the grandson of the greatest man who had ever lived at that time; the grandson of the man with whom God talked with face to face?

Some editions tell us that he was the grandson of a man called Manasseh, but most manuscripts say Moses. The rabbi's say that there is an 'n' set over the heading of the name which means that the 'n' sound should be left out. If that is correct, then it spells Moses, who indeed had a son called Gershom. How sad then that it seems that it was a grandson of Moses that would turn into such an opportunist type of Minister to the point where he would infect a whole tribe with idolatry. Sadly, he's not the only example of a great man's posterity degenerating over the years. Children's children are not always the crown of old men!

What then are the lessons that we can draw from this story. The heart of this story is about the faults of a Minister who has essentially put himself out for hire. He has 'followed the money' instead of following the Lord. He has become the proverbial 'hireling' that Jesus warned us about when He talked about Himself being the good shepherd. He said, *"The hireling sees the wolf coming and leaves the sheep and flees. He flees because he is a hireling and does not care about the sheep."* This story is indicative of Ministers who leave their pastorates as soon as something 'better' comes along. This story is also a reflection of those Ministers who will quickly leave their churches to follow their large financial supporters and in effect, become their private priests.

Lastly, we learn that when a people fall away from God, the work of God becomes mixed with other entities and the ministry of the Holy Spirit becomes adulterated with seducing, religious spirits. The tribe of Dan paid for that and so will we if we mix the demonic with the Divine!

Rejected Ministers

The Bible reveals the final outcome of many of God's people who brought their lives under His judgement and sadly, some of those people were in one way or another, Ministers of God. The penalties for polluting the ministry have been heavy and sometimes very swift. The two sons of Aaron who ministered in the Tabernacle were instantly consumed by fire when they glibly entered the Holy Place and offered fire and incense that the Lord had not commanded. They were guilty of the sins of presumption and self-will and it caused them to dishonor the sanctity of the ministry. They forgot that as the Ministers of God, they were literally and proverbially carrying 'hot coals of fire' and so fire came from the Lord and consumed them! In a moment, they were gone!

'By those who come near Me I must be regarded as holy' said the Lord.

In this chapter I want to take a look at three men whom God rejected. They all lived in Old Testament times but the New Testament still warns us that even in a 'Day of Grace' there will be people just like them! Characters just like them were among the Early Church believers and they will most certainly be in the Church in the Last Days. This chapter therefore is a very important one for us because of the times that we are now living in.

It's very difficult to write with any authority on the subject of the 'End Times' because so much of it is up for debate! There are many end-time scenarios, all of which have scriptural support; so how can anyone really present a view of the 'end of the age' without it being scripturally challenged. Having said that, it does seem that there are some things that everyone can agree on. Everyone believes that Jesus *will* return and that He will judge the nations severely. Before that event, there will come a man whose world leadership will have been characterized by cruel control, hate and violence against many. He is often referred to as the *'Anti-Christ' – the one who is against Christ or the one who usurps the place of Christ.* He will of course reflect both of these aspects. The New Testament describes him as 'the man of sin' or 'the man of lawlessness.' The evil spirit that will come into this man's life has already been around for a long time and it will remain under God's restraint until this man arrives on the scene and *then* it will find its full manifestation in him –the 'son of perdition' who is eternally doomed. At the end of the age, he will take center-stage in world affairs but there is something that happens before he arrives that sets the scene for him. What is that something? It's an apostate Christian Church on a worldwide scale!

2 Thessalonians 2:1-4

'Now, brethren, concerning the coming of our Lord Jesus Christ and our gathering together to Him, we ask you, not to be shaken in mind or troubled, either by spirit or by word or by letter, as if from us, as though the day of Christ had come. Let no one deceive you by any means; for that Day will not come unless the falling away comes first, and the man of sin is revealed, the son of perdition,

*who opposes and exalts himself above all that is called God or that
is worshiped, so that he sits as God in the temple of God, showing
himself that he is God.*

The Anti-Christ is God's judgment on an unbelieving
world that did not receive the 'love of the truth' and who
chose to reject the Gospel of Jesus Christ; willfully filling
their lives with the pleasures of unrighteousness. The
apostle Paul told Timothy that the Holy Spirit had spoken
strongly to him about the end of the age; how that some will
depart from the faith having been deceived by evil spirits
and philosophies of demons.

To our shame, the stage for this terrible person will be
made through the apostasy of many who call themselves
Christians. *What does 'apostasy' mean? It means 'to stand away
from' – it's an act of rebelling, forsaking and abandoning that which
you once believed.* The Old Testament phrase which Paul used
was *'a falling away.'*

What this means is that the generations preceding the
coming of the Anti-Christ will be increasingly made up
of those who have departed from the faith. It's not that
Christianity as a world religion will disappear. No, not at all;
Christianity will continue having a 'form of godliness' but it
will have very little *true* experience of God's Holy Spirit. The
Church of the Last Days will be like the church at Laodicea
who thought that they were doing well; but they were in fact
miserable, poor, blind and naked before the Lord. So, the
spiritual atmosphere in the last days will be one of apostasy
and it will be the apostasy of the Church that sets the stage
for the 'man of sin' for when the 'salt has lost its saltiness'
what good is it? When we are no longer a light to the world,
can we expect anything else but encroaching darkness?

The book of Jude is an epistle that warns us of apostasies past and present. In that regard, I think that it's placed perfectly in the New Testament just before the revealing of Jesus Christ to the world. He warns the people of his day that certain ungodly men have crept into the church unnoticed and have persuaded people away from the doctrines of Christ and from living a holy life.

He goes on to say how God dealt with people like that before when He brought His own people out of Egypt; but then destroyed all those who provoked Him to anger and who did not believe, even after seeing so many mighty miracles. He even talks about those angels who in the early days of humanity, left their spiritual places; took on flesh and bred giants in the world; how that God has put them in eternal chains under darkness until Judgment Day. He also mentioned the people of Sodom and Gomorrah; how they perverted themselves and how they suffered the vengeance of eternal fire. Then Jude goes on to give three examples of men who represented all of those ungodly people who had crept in unnoticed. The irony is that all three were well-acquainted with the ministry of God.

Jude v11

'Woe to them! For they have gone in the way of Cain, have run greedily in the error of Balaam for profit, and perished in the rebellion of Korah.'

The Way of Cain

In the Last Days, many are going to go in the way of Cain. What was the way of Cain?

Genesis 4:1-5

'Now Adam knew Eve his wife, and she conceived and bore Cain, and said, "I have acquired a man from the Lord." Then she bore again, this time his brother Abel. Now Abel was a keeper of sheep, but Cain was a tiller of the ground.

And in the process of time it came to pass that Cain brought an offering of the fruit of the ground to the Lord. Abel also brought of the firstborn of his flock and of their fat. And the Lord respected Abel and his offering, but He did not respect Cain and his offering, and his countenance fell.'

The Scriptures say in Proverbs *'that there is a way that seems right unto a man but the end of that way is death.'*

Why didn't God respect Cain and his offering? Cain didn't deny the existence of God. Cain was a believer. He wasn't refusing to worship God. Both Cain and Abel were allowed to approach God and minister to Him through the offerings that they had placed before Him. The Lord accepted Abel's offering but rejected Cain's. So what was wrong with Cain's offering?

Hebrews 11 is the key that unlocks the door to our understanding.

Hebrews 11:4

'By faith Abel offered to God a more excellent sacrifice than Cain, through which he obtained witness that he was righteous, God testifying of his gifts; and through it he being dead still speaks.'

Abel offered to God *something* that Cain didn't and in *a way* that Cain didn't. First, Abel offered a blood sacrifice for his acceptance and secondly, he did this in faith believing that it was God's revealed way. *'Faith comes by hearing the word of God.'* In other words, faith is an action performed in view of what God has revealed! Had God revealed to Cain and Abel the necessity of a sacrificial covering? Yes, He had -when the Lord clothed their parents with the skins of innocent animals. Furthermore, He had spoken to their parents about the promise of a Man that would come and redeem everything that they had lost to the Serpent; that is the Devil. So, both men knew that the way to acceptance with God was a life-sacrifice. Both men knew the divine protocols that had been instituted, but Cain *'stepped away from that'* and brought to God the fruit of his *own* works out of the ground that the Lord had cursed. Cain's confidence was in himself and in his own works. Abel gave an offering 'by faith' -according to the revelation of God but Cain totally bypassed the substitutionary nature of the 'life's blood of another' for acceptable fellowship with God.

So what is the way of Cain? It's to live a life for God entirely by your *own* works. Cain was a believer who went his *own* way! The ultimate consequences of that were dire because he later rose up and killed his brother and Cain who once had the ear of God was rejected by Him.

For Christians to 'go in the way of Cain' –it means that they are not receiving God's grace and favor because they are attempting to win God's approval through the strength of their *own* efforts. This is very offensive to God because it bypasses the blood sacrifice of His Son on the Cross and undermines the complete and perfect work that He did to save men.

But the subtlety of 'the way of Cain' lies not in regard to our concept of personal salvation; its subtlety lies in our concept of *service* to God! Therefore, it's possible to lead a church in Christian things and yet be without God! It's possible to run a missionary organization without the Holy Spirit being involved at all! And it's possible to be a believer in Jesus Christ and yet fill your life with only the things that *you* want to do; bypass the Holy Spirit in His authority; ignore the authority of the Scriptures; refuse to take up your cross and then convince yourself that 'it is well with your soul!' How scary is that!

This is a huge temptation that comes to us all because we don't want to *have* to trust God. There's a big difference between believing in God and *having* to trust in Him –that's a place we try to avoid if we can. None of us want to be 'up against the wall' and be without contingencies. What a nightmare it is for us in these times to run out of options! But faith requires risk –that's just the way it is. So, to please God you learn *not* to depend on yourself but upon hearing His voice! It's obedience to *His* revelation in your life that gains His respect and grants your reward. Hearing God requires a true heart relationship with Him and as you grow in His grace, you hear His voice and consequently you grow in faith.

Some Christians have been deceived into thinking that faith is *all* you need. That's not correct because faith is not what comes first. What comes first is God's voice to you –and *then* faith comes into your heart. Some Christians believe that all they need to do for successful living is to learn wisdom through the laws and principles of God that are revealed in the Bible. Sadly, they have been deceived into going the 'way of Cain' because they are trusting in *themselves* to successfully implement *their* faith in the laws of God for *their* ministry. Implementation of Biblical, spiritual laws *can* bring success into your life because His word is truth; but true blessings come through *His* grace and favor upon you. True blessings in your life are those blessings which *He* grants to you! The Bible says: *'For it is God who works in you both to will and to do for His good pleasure.'*

The Church at the end of this present age will be full of believers who have gone the way of Cain! Woe to them! They will get the shock of their lives at the end. The best scenario that can be afforded to them is that they may be saved through the fire of the Judgement Seat of Christ! Their works will go up in a cloud of smoke, for there will be no rewards for those who go in the 'way of Cain.' How can there be rewards when God has clearly rejected those kinds of offerings? The apostate Church that leads to the Anti-Christ will be full of people who believe in God but don't know Him or His ways!

Woe to them! Woe to them because they have sought to do the work of God *their* way instead of following the Divine protocols of the Cross upon their lives and ministry.

The Error of Balaam
Jude v11

'*Woe to them who have ran greedily in the error of Balaam for profit.*'

Balaam was a prophet of the Lord in Old Testament times. He was no phony –he had the goods. He knew God and to a certain degree 'walked with God.' He was wonderfully gifted in visions and in prophecy and moreover, he had power with God in that whom he blessed was blessed and whom he cursed was cursed.

But he had a weakness. He loved money. He was taken up with the things of this world and to put it bluntly, he prostituted his gifts and abilities from God to get wealth for himself. He was a prophet for hire; a Minister of God for a fee. His covetousness ran deep and it was only a matter of time before his obsession for money and civil honors would get the better of him.

King Balak of Moab hired him to curse the Children of Israel when they were passing through his territory which ironically, was totally unnecessary. God had already commanded them not to take any of the land of Moab for He had given it to the descendants of Lot, Abraham's nephew, as a possession. A great sense of dread had overtaken the Moabites when the Children of Israel encamped in the area and so the leaders of the people went to ask Balaam to come and curse the families of Jacob; offering him money for his ministry services.

Well, Balaam tried to curse God's people but soon discovered that he couldn't because God commanded him as His prophet to bless Israel. Balaam therefore had to leave the scene and walk away from the reward that he had been offered from King Balak of the Moabites.

But because he loved money more than God, he thought again, and he told the King of Moab to tempt the men of Israel to mix with the Moabite women; join in their feasts and festivals; have sex with them and worship their gods. This they did. Many of the Children of Israel broke their covenant relationship with God and they died in the ensuing plague; but Balaam no doubt got his money! It was *his* teaching that caused all that!

Revelation 2:14

'But I have a few things against you, because you have there those who hold the doctrine of Balaam, who taught Balak to put a stumbling block before the children of Israel, to eat things sacrificed to idols, and to commit sexual immorality.'

The apostle Peter also warned the people of his day that there would be folks just like Balaam among them and will remain so until the 'Day of the Lord' when He will come as a thief in the night.

2 Peter 2:14-16

'Having eyes full of adultery and that cannot cease from sin, enticing unstable souls. They have a heart trained in covetous practices, and are accursed children. They have forsaken the right way and gone astray, following the way of Balaam the son of Beor, who loved the wages of unrighteousness; but he was rebuked for his iniquity: a dumb donkey speaking with a man's voice restrained the madness of the prophet.'

The Church in the Last Days will be full of believers who have gone the way of Balaam! Woe to them! Woe to those Ministers who hire themselves out for profit and for personal aggrandizement. Woe to those Ministers whose hearts are set not on delivering the Word of God but on their remuneration of it! Woe to those Ministers who will not visit a church unless there is a large sum of money given up front; then use the church facilities and staff to promote their materials and then take up a special offering for themselves at the end of the week! Woe to them! For their heart is trained in covetous practices. Just like the Pharisees in Jesus' day, they are lovers of money and they have forsaken the right way and gone astray, following the way of Balaam. Before the first advent of the Lord Jesus, God asked His back-slidden Ministers the question: *"Will a man rob God?"* It seems that before the second advent of the Lord Jesus that God will still be asking the same question! The Minister's attitude towards his personal money and his handling of the Lord's money is most certainly like 'carrying hot coals of fire.'

The Rebellion of Korah
Jude v11

'Woe to them who have gone in the rebellious way of Korah.'

Who was Korah? Korah was a Levite. He was a cousin of Moses.

Numbers 16:1-5

'Now Korah the son of Izhar, the son of Kohath, the son of Levi, with Dathan and Abiram the sons of Eliab, and On the son of Peleth, the sons of Reuben, took men; and they rose up before Moses with some of the children of Israel, two hundred and fifty leaders of the congregation, representatives of the congregation, men of renown.

They gathered together against Moses and Aaron, and said to them, "You take too much upon yourselves, for all the congregation is holy, every one of them, and the Lord is among them. Why then do you exalt yourselves above the assembly of the Lord?"

So when Moses heard it, he fell on his face; and he spoke to Korah and all his company, saying, "Tomorrow morning the Lord will show who is His and who is holy, and will cause him to come near to Him. That one whom He chooses He will cause to come near to Him.

Despite all the evidences that God had chosen Moses to lead the people and that his brother Aaron had clearly been appointed by God to be the high priest, with his sons alone constituting the priesthood; there arose some Levites and others from among the congregation that objected to being under their rule.

They took a singular truth out of context and used it to rebel against the leaders that God had set up. They saw that in God's eyes, the whole congregation was holy before the Lord and that every individual was also holy. All of this was true. The Lord spoke to Moses face to face but He could also speak in one way or another to *any* of His people. (Today we would call this truth –'the priesthood of the believer.') However, God had set Moses and Aaron *over* the congregation as His representatives and so a rebellion against them was a rebellion against Him! Korah mustered two hundred and fifty leaders of the people and along with others they gathered against Moses and Aaron. When Moses heard what Korah was saying he fell on his face –never a good sign! It didn't end well. Korah and his rebellious colleagues, along with everything they owned fell down alive into Hell; the earth itself opening up around their tents and then closing up after they had gone! As for the two hundred and fifty leaders who had risen up against Moses and Aaron, they were also slain in a moment when the fire of the Lord burst upon them!

So what is the way of Korah? The way of Korah is the way of rebellion. Rebellion against what? Rebellion against God's appointed leaders by using the freedom that comes to the individual believer to circumvent leadership authority in their lives. In political terms, it is to introduce and promote a selfish democracy into a theocratic environment. The news for this generation is that the Kingdom of God is *not* a democracy. There's no such thing in Heaven as 'majority rule.' In Heaven they all know who's on the Throne and in the invisible world of demon spirits; they too know who's in charge! It seems that we're the only ones that don't get it! Because we've drank deeply from the 'chalice' of Greek philosophy, many believers to-day are simply ignorant of the ramifications of usurping God's appointed leaders. The Ministers of Christ are not only God-appointed; they are God-anointed. If people in their congregations should ever rise up against them in a defiant way, they are probably unaware that they are touching the anointing of the Holy Spirit -which for them is a dangerous thing!

It's not to say that Christian leadership has no accountability or that it can't even be removed if warranted; but if we really understood this, there would be many ugly situations that just wouldn't develop. But how many times have disgruntled congregants leaned on Church Board members to just flatly, get rid of the pastor? In moments like that, the malcontents should be brought into a fair but searching question and answer situation, like as follows: "Why should we get rid of the pastor? Has he been having an affair?" "No." "Has been stealing money from the church?" "No." "Has been teaching wrong doctrine?" "No."

"Why then?" "Well, we just feel that the church is going nowhere and there's nothing really happening. It's like we have no vision and I just think we need a change." "But aren't you the ones who've said that 'You're fed up with all these 'career pastors' who come in and then fly out as soon as they're offered something better?' Haven't you all made comments on how these pastors offer no stability – like they can't stick with anything?!"

The Church in the Last Days will be full of disgruntled people who will rise up against God's appointed leaders; those, whom the Scriptures say, *'Have the rule over them in the Lord'* and rebel against their persons and their preaching. I say their preaching because the phrase used here in Jude is *'the gainsaying of Korah.'* The Greek word that is used is 'antilogia' which means 'against the word.' The Church in the Last Days will be full of rebellious Christians who will not come under the authority of the preached word. They will be constantly contradicting what the preachers have said to them from platforms and pulpits. Rejecting the true

Ministers and their words, they will deceive themselves into bypassing regular church attendance altogether. Woe to them! For they have gone in the rebellious way of Korah!

Cain, Balaam and Korah

The spiritual slide that we have seen over the last century and indeed we are both part and victim of it now; will get worse and worse until by the end of the age it will lead to a *super* apostasy. Each of these men portrays a particular aspect of 'falling away' or 'standing away' from the truth. Jude has not recorded them in chronological order but they are in a prophetic order of spiritual decay. In Cain, we have a farmer, a tiller of the soil. In Balaam we have a prophet and in Korah we have a prince in Israel. In these three, we can see the lamentable path of apostasy.

Those who go in the way of Cain do the ministry in their flesh; only doing those things that play to their strengths and are aliens to the Cross of Christ; not experiencing His power being made perfect in their weakness and not understanding that it is through faith and trust in His Word that God is well-pleased.

Those who go in the way of Balaam do everything in life and in ministry for money or for some form of personal gain. Jude describes them as 'wandering stars' –people who are disengaged from God's heavenly purposes and are roaming around seeking to do ministry for profit. And when they see opportunities where personal advancement can be made, they set their sights and they run greedily towards the target. Unlike Moses, they esteem the treasures of Egypt more than the approval of God.

Those who go in the way of Korah seek through their own individualism to reject or even overthrow the Ministers and the preaching that comes to them; clothing themselves in robes of Christian liberty. But deep down, they resent being preached to and if they *have* to be part of God's family somewhere; if *some* sort of fellowship becomes a pressing need in their lives; they'd rather go to a 'church' in a coffee-house where everyone can a sit in a circle and just share with one another. They can turn up there anytime they like, wear whatever they like and keep everything on a casual level. And the 'icing on the cake' for them will be that no one in the room has been authorized to bring the Word of God to bear on their consciences!

If we go in the way of Cain, we will disconnect ourselves from God and put *our* way before God's revealed Word. And if we do that over many years, we will learn how to do ministry *without* God and we will constantly seek better opportunities for ourselves; and compensation for what we do will become more and more important. Eventually, money and position will steal our hearts and we will run hard after them both! This is the way of Balaam.

And if we allow ourselves to be caught in that net, we will eventually rebel against all godly teaching and counsel, and we will become like the rebellious fool in Proverbs when it says, *"He who is often reproved and yet hardens his neck, will suddenly be destroyed and that without remedy!"*

It's difficult to have any hope for people like this because any plain reading of the epistles of Jude and Peter will show that all apostates are doomed! The apostle Paul confirms it boldly, saying that God will send those who did not continue in the way of the Lord a strong delusion so that they may be condemned with the world, because they did not believe or receive the love of the truth but had pleasure in unrighteousness. They chose the 'pleasures of sin for a season.'

Should such as these be saved? Should those who have lived like the world and have refused to carry the reproach of Christ in this life receive eternal rewards? The Bible says No! The Anti-Christ will be their reward for by their ways, they have prepared the world for him! By their ways, they have effectively rejected Biblical absolutes and have made the world into the bowl of putrid soup that it certainly will be at that time.

However, for the true Minister; for the true Christian; for the true lover of the truth as it is in Jesus –Jude says these words: *"But you, beloved, building yourselves up on your most holy faith, praying in the Holy Spirit, keep yourselves in the love of God, looking for the mercy of our Lord Jesus Christ unto eternal life."*

"Now unto Him who is able to keep you from falling away, (Him who is able to keep you from apostasy and from the strong delusion that He will send upon the world,) *and is able to present you faultless before the Presence of His glory, with exceeding joy: To God our Savior, who alone is wise, be glory and majesty, dominion and power, both now and forever, Amen!"*

The Men of Anathoth

Before we begin our study on the 'men of Anathoth' let us first understand what Anathoth is and how it came about. Anathoth was a city in the land of Benjamin, getting its name no doubt from a grandson of Benjamin –the eighth grandson of nine, Anathoth.

The city of Anathoth was one of four cities in the land of Benjamin that were set aside for the tribe of Levi. (The Levites were not given land allotments. They were given cities and the common area fields around those cities.) In the process of time, Anathoth became not only a city for the Levites but also for the priests of the Lord. So, Anathoth was a priest city and it was located about three miles from Jerusalem. That short distance made the priests work in the Temple quite accessible.

Between Anathoth and Jerusalem there had been a previous city of priests called Nob. After the Lord had destroyed Shiloh, where the Tabernacle had originally been set up; the priests and their families settled in the city of Nob. But, there was a dark, spiritual cloud hanging over them. The shadow of God's judgment was cast over them because their forefathers, Eli and his two sons, had disgraced themselves in the ministry and God had told Eli through a prophet and young Samuel that He was going to kill his two sons and take away the honor of the priesthood from his line; that his high priesthood calling would be given to another branch of the family of Aaron.

Eli and his Sons
1 Samuel 2:27-35

'Then a man of God came to Eli and said to him, "Thus says the Lord: 'Did I not clearly reveal Myself to the house of your father when they were in Egypt in Pharaoh's house?' Did I not choose him out of all the tribes of Israel to be My priest, to offer upon My altar, to burn incense, and to wear an ephod before Me? And did I not give to the house of your father all the offerings of the children of Israel made by fire?

'Why do you kick at My sacrifice and My offering which I have commanded in My dwelling place, and honor your sons more than Me, to make yourselves fat with the best of all the offerings of Israel, My people?'

"Therefore the Lord God of Israel says: 'I said indeed that your house and the house of your father would walk before Me forever.' But now the Lord says: 'Far be it from Me; for those who honor Me I will honor, and those who despise Me shall be lightly esteemed. 'Behold the days are coming that I will cut off your arm and the arm of your father's house, so that there will not be an old man in your house.

'And you will see an enemy in My dwelling place, despite all the good which God does for Israel. And there shall not be an old man in your house forever. 'But any of your men whom I do not cut off from My altar shall consume your eyes and grieve your heart. And all the descendants of your house shall die in the flower of their age. 'Now this shall be a sign to you that will come upon your two sons, on Hophni and Phinehas: in one day they shall die, both of them.

'Then I will raise up for Myself a faithful priest who shall do according to what is in My heart and in My mind. I will build him a sure house, and he shall walk before My anointed forever.'"

Shortly after that, the nation went to war with the Philistines and the battle went against them and about four thousand men were killed. Thinking that the Ark of the Covenant would bring the Lord Himself to the battle front; they took it out of its hallowed place and brought it into the camp with great shouts of joy from the soldiers. The Philistines fought them again and won the day decisively and they marched home with the ark of God! A man who had been on the front line ran all the way to Shiloh and told the terrible news to everyone. He came running up to Eli and told him also what had taken place in that his two sons had been killed in the battle and that the ark of God had been captured. Eli was stunned by the news, lost his balance and fell off his seat; broke his neck and died. In one day, everything concerning Eli had been taken away. The word of the Lord was fulfilled in them when all three lost their lives within hours of each other. Furthermore, it would seem that Shiloh itself was destroyed at that time; making a further break in what had been the recognized priesthood of Eli and his sons.

Eli was from the lineage of Ithamar and so from that moment on, all the priests who could trace their line to Eli and Ithamar were on 'borrowed time' as far as their *preeminence* in the priesthood went. After the destruction of Shiloh as a location for the Tabernacle, the remaining priests and their families moved to a city in the territory of Benjamin, called Nob. There they continued to live and serve the ministry of God but the day came when they met a despicable man called Doeg the Edomite. This man had seen David at Nob when he had come to seek out Ahimelech the priest, and he had seen David receiving assistance from him. Doeg was a servant of King Saul and he told Saul all about the things he had observed. Under the orders of King Saul, Doeg killed all the priests and the people at Nob –or so he thought. One of them escaped. His name was Abiathar and he escaped with the sacred ephod and came to David when he was hiding from King Saul at the cave of Adullam. David was happy to receive him and thereafter, Abiathar served David as high-priest. Abiathar was the 11th high priest from Aaron and David caused him to share the high-priesthood with Zadok; who was also a direct descendant of Aaron, only through Eleazar and not Ithamar.

When David established himself as King over all Israel, Abiathar and the family of priests attached to him lived in Anathoth. Anathoth was *their* city and they had common area fields for their fruits and vegetables and for their livestock.

Abiathar and Zadok

Abiathar was loyal to David all through his reign; even during the time of Absalom's rebellion. However after David died, despite the fact that God had said to David that his son Solomon would inherit the throne; Solomon's elder brother Adonijah made a bid for the crown and Abiathar supported his claim. He backed the wrong man. He threw his support around Adonijah and not Solomon, whom *God* had appointed to be king after David. Solomon came to the throne because it was of the Lord; and it was Zadok the priest that had remained loyal to him and to the revealed will of God. As for Abiathar the priest, from the family tree of Eli, the 'shadow' of God's prophetic word was still 'clouding the skies' of both him and his whole priestly line. When Solomon eventually became king, he dealt quite sharply with the enemies of both him and his father David. After giving his brother Adonijah a reprieve, it was discovered that he was still vying for the throne and so Solomon had him executed for treason. Then he had to decide what to do with his 'turbulent priest' Abiathar and the Bible tells us what he said and what he did.

1 Kings 2:26-27

'And to Abiathar the priest the king said, "Go to Anathoth, to your own fields, for you are deserving of death; but I will not put you to death at this time, because you carried the ark of the Lord God before my father David, and because you were afflicted every time my father was afflicted."

So Solomon removed Abiathar from being priest to the Lord, that he might fulfill the word of the Lord which He spoke concerning the house of Eli at Shiloh.'

The 'end of the line' had come for the preeminence of the house of Eli and Zadok was then set apart to become the sole high-priest. Zadok was that faithful priest that the Lord told Eli that He would raise up, and Zadok's descendants had that requisite 'nobility' in them; for they continued as priests well into the intertestamental period. The prophet Ezekiel declared that during the time of the exile the only faithful ones were the sons of Zadok!

Abiathar escaped with his life and he was sent back to his city; living out the rest of his days with his brethren priests in the city of Anathoth. Abiathar had lost his position and as a consequence, *so did the rest of his priestly family* and more importantly, they'd lost the favor of God. All was not well in the ministry in Anathoth!

So, here we have a city of priests –'the men of Anathoth.' They'd been first for a long time –but now they were very much, second. When people who have been at the top become 'crest-fallen' it hurts! The men of Anathoth were still in the ministry, but they would never be 'Number One' again! They were now destined to serve the Lord under the leadership of the sons of Zadok.

Thankfully, God's grace can be greater than His judgment at times. Doesn't the Scriptures tell us that *'mercy rejoices against judgment'*? God's mercy was never taken away from them and He brought out from among them one of the greatest prophets to have ever lived! His name was Jeremiah. When God called Jeremiah, he was a young man and he was from the family of priests living at Anathoth.

Jeremiah the Prophet
Jeremiah 1:1-3

'The words of Jeremiah the son of Hilkiah, of the priests who were in Anathoth in the land of Benjamin, to whom the word of the Lord came in the days of Josiah the son of Amon, king of Judah, in the thirteenth year of his reign. It came also in the days of Jehoiakim the son of Josiah, king of Judah, until the end of the eleventh year of Zedekiah the son of Josiah, king of Judah, until the carrying away of Jerusalem captive in the fifth month.'

Jeremiah's ministry was to last over forty years and many troubles came his way during that time. However, what are in focus for us in this chapter are the events surrounding the earliest days of his work for God. Jeremiah soon found that the words he was declaring from God were contrary to what the other prophets were saying. Consequently, his ministry caused a lot of friction and he made many enemies in Jerusalem and throughout the nation. He would discover quite quickly that it's one thing to have enemies that are foreign and another to have enemies that are domestic! It's much more difficult when your enemies are those of your *own* household!

That's unfortunately where the 'men of Anathoth' come in to the picture. His own brothers; Ministers of God; priests of the Lord and men of his home town, became his enemy –proving once again, that *'a prophet has no honor in his own country.'*

You would have thought that the men of Anathoth would have been very proud of him; for there in Jerusalem was one of their own, boldly declaring the word of the Lord! But that wasn't what happened. What happened was that they got angry with him and no doubt jealous of his ministry and they chose to *secretly* fight against him; stirring up the mob against him and threatening him with his life if he continued. Jeremiah, being young and possible a little naïve, didn't know what was really going on because when his brothers talked with him, they all sounded fine to him. But God gave him 'revelation knowledge' as to what his brothers and the 'men of Anathoth' were *really* doing. They were in fact plotting his downfall.

Jeremiah 11:18-23

'Now the Lord gave me knowledge of it, and I know it; for You showed me their doings. But I was like a docile lamb brought to the slaughter; and I did not know that they had devised schemes against me, saying, "Let us destroy the tree with its fruit, and let us cut him off from the land of the living, that his name may be remembered no more."

But, O Lord of hosts, You who judge righteously, testing the mind and the heart, Let me see your vengeance on them, for to You I have revealed my cause.

"Therefore thus says the Lord concerning the men of Anathoth who seek your life, saying, 'Do not prophesy in the name of the Lord, lest you die by our hand' –"therefore thus says the Lord of hosts: "Behold I will punish them. The young men shall die by the

sword, their sons and their daughters shall die by famine; 'and there shall be no remnant of them, for I will bring catastrophe on the men of Anathoth, even the year of their punishment.'"

The men of his home town were against him *and* the ministry that God had given him. It would have been a little easier to bear were it not for the fact that this animosity ran so deep that even Jeremiah's brothers were of the same mind.

Jeremiah 12:6

'For even your brothers, the house of your father, even they have dealt treacherously with you; Yes, they have called a multitude after you. Do not believe them, even though they speak smooth words to you.'

Jealousy in the Ministry

What is this topic saying to us to-day? It is telling us that there always seems to be a lot of 'flesh' in the lives of the Ministers of God. The Ministers of God are human beings like everyone else; it's just that one expects certain standards of behavior from those who represent the Lord.

It's always a sad day when we see jealousy raise its ugly head and there's a deeper grief when it's found in the hearts of those who hold spiritual authority in the Church. Envy can produce all manner of hurt and there's no arena of life where it cannot find a home if left unattended. Not only can we find it within our own circle of friends we can even encounter it within our own households!

Wasn't this Joseph's problem? He was set apart by his father and given a 'coat of many colors' and his brothers couldn't handle it; dismissing him as 'a dreamer.' Of all the dangers that Joseph walked through it was his brothers who came the closest to killing him. Wasn't this also the Lord's problem when early on in His ministry, He visited His home town of Nazareth; and were it not for the intervention of God, they would have thrown Him off the cliff! Of all the dangers the Lord walked through, and there were many; it was the 'men of Nazareth' that came the closest to killing Him!

Jealousy leads to rejection and rejection can lead to hate! Jealousy in the ministry has got to be one of the Devil's *favorite* tools. One of the reasons that it's a 'weapon of choice' is because through *jealousy* he can get up close and deeply personal. He loves to fight at close quarters if he can!

The 'men of Anathoth' —here are the main lessons for us.

First, let us never become like *them*! Let us never allow *our* hearts to become like *theirs* to where we will fight a genuine brother or sister in the Lord. Secondly, if you *are* that genuine brother or sister; if you are a 'Jeremiah,' try not to react and allow God to take care of them.

The Ministry can be a very competitive place and you will find that Ministers who easily become jealous of others all drink out of the same 'poisoned chalice' - the one labeled 'Comparison.'

Once you drink the 'sour wine of comparison' you begin a downward spiral that leads to depression and begins a gloomy dejection which eventually has you running for the exits! Yes, 'Comparison' can cause you to quit!

So let us all take heed to ourselves so that we don't fall into the traps of jealousy; and find ourselves behaving just like the 'men of Anathoth' who crest-fallen themselves couldn't stand not being number one anymore.

On a personal note, I believe that I saw this dynamic played out right in front of me one day at a zoo of all places. My brother Mark and I were at the Islamorada Zoo in the Florida Keys, part of which was used for a wild bird show.

We sat in the crowd and watched with amazement the things that many of the exotic birds could do. They would squawk, perform, poop and then eat the nuts that the trainer gave them. Each bird had its own 'party-piece' but as usual, the trainer saved the best bird 'til last! The final bird was a fine specimen with bright colors and being the oldest bird there, he had the best tricks. As he began to give the crowd the best performance of the afternoon, it was what happened next that really got my attention. As he began to -as they say, "Knock it out of the park" the other birds went crazy. I am no bird expert but it seemed to me that they were all jealous of his superlative abilities because they squawked so loud all the time he was performing! It became quite deafening at one point and it really did look like they were having a hard time not being the center of attention! They had been good at what they did, but he was better. I thought to myself, "Oh my goodness, even in the world of birds, jealousy cannot abide someone else excelling!"

If the Apostle Paul was still with us he would say these words for the benefit of all present-day Ministers of Christ: *'For we dare not class ourselves or compare ourselves with those who commend themselves. But they, measuring themselves by themselves, and comparing themselves among themselves, are not wise. We, however, will not boast beyond measure, but within the limits of the sphere which God appointed us. But he who glories, let him glory in the Lord; for not he who commends himself is approved, but whom the Lord commends.'*

Saul s Spear

Some time ago, my wife Pauline told me that when reading her Bible, how taken she had been with King Saul and his spear. She gave me many thoughts concerning that spear in his life and so I studied the subject for myself and I'd like to share what I believe the Lord would say about this to us all and in particular, what He would say to His Ministers. Let's take a look then at Saul and his spear.

First of all, I think we must first appreciate what symbolic power the 'king's spear' possessed in the history of Israel and thereby ascertain the thought patterns of their minds. If you will recall, it was Joshua and *his* spear that God used to win the victory over the enemy. Let's visit that moment in the Scriptures.

Joshua 8:18-19 & v25-26

'Then the Lord said to Joshua, "Stretch out the spear that is in your hand toward Ai, for I will give it into your hand." And Joshua stretched out the spear that was in his hand toward the city. So those in ambush arose quickly out of their place; they ran as soon as he had stretched out his hand, and they entered the city and took it, and hurried to set the city on fire.

So it was that all who fell that day, both men and women were twelve thousand —all the people of Ai. For Joshua did not draw back his hand, with which he stretched out the spear, until he had utterly destroyed all the inhabitants of Ai.'

God used the symbolic, intercessory power of Joshua and his spear to wage war against the city of Ai; just like He'd previously used the rod of God in the hands of Moses in intercessory power over the Amalekites.

It's apparent then, that the 'king's spear' in Saul's hand would reflect the symbolic aura of the 'rod of God' giving him the Divine right to exercise authority as monarch of the people. The 'spear' signified his right to rule and his power to act as the nation's sovereign. It was a very important piece of regal equipment, having an inherent mystical quality about it and he always kept it near him.

(We have great difficulty now accepting so much power being placed in the hands of one man, but such was the power of a monarch. Many years later, God would give this kind of power to a man called Nebuchadnezzar who was king of Babylon and of the known world at that time. God gave him absolute power over peoples, nations and languages and whomever he wished, he executed and whomever he wished, he kept alive.)

The Calling of Saul

After Joshua died, the Lord raised up judges in Israel to deliver them from their enemies and to subsequently rule over them. They were chosen by God at His pleasure and they governed the people through the anointing of the Holy Spirit which came upon them. But then the people asked for a king; which wasn't the best thing for them, but God allowed it and He chose a wonderful young man called Saul.

He was a good choice for he was a man of great quality. What was most notable about him was the fact that he stood head and shoulders above everyone else and if that wasn't enough, he was also the best-looking man in the kingdom! Saul was the best that Israel had to offer and God gave His people the best there was at that time.

The prophet Samuel came into his life, anointed his head with oil and the Spirit of God came upon him from that day onwards. Shortly after that, he was crowned king and invested with all his royal privileges and prerogatives. He received a crown upon his head to signify his anointing from God which at the same time gave him the Divine right to rule and command all of the Lord's people.

God set Saul up perfectly but he lost his way with the Lord and he made a mess of his life and ministry; disobeying the commands of the Lord. It left the Lord with no other choice but to reject him and to look for someone else who *would* fulfill His purposes. Consequently, there *was* a turning point in Saul's life and ministry.

1 Samuel 13:13-14

'And Samuel said to Saul, "You have done foolishly. You have not kept the commandment of the Lord your God, which He commanded you. For now the Lord would have established your kingdom over Israel forever. But now your kingdom shall not continue. The Lord has sought for Himself a man after His own heart, and the Lord has commanded him to be commander over His people, because you have not kept what the Lord commanded you."

From the moment those prophetic words were declared over Saul and his kingdom, things went badly for him. Only his son Jonathan was a bright light in his very dark sky. The black clouds of anxiety and depression were gathering around him and erratic behavior was soon an everyday experience for Saul and his family.

King Saul had now become like Samson who asleep on the knees of his lover had the Spirit of God leave him. Saul was still in office but the power had gone, for when God sees that the 'power has gone *to* your head' He takes the 'power *off* your head.' Samson lost his anointing and Saul did too. God looked for another man's head to anoint with fresh oil and He found His servant, David.

The Anointing of David
1 Samuel 16:13-14

'Then Samuel took the horn of oil and anointed him in the midst of his brothers; and the Spirit of the Lord came upon David from that day forward. So Samuel arose and went to Ramah.

But the Spirit of the Lord departed from Saul, and a distressing spirit from the Lord troubled him.'

This is the day of the 'great switch' when one man falls and another rises.

God removed His Spirit *off* Saul and put His Spirit *on* young David. God is not the 'author of confusion' and so He doesn't anoint two kings at the same time. He can anoint many people with complimentary gifts at one time, but not two kings; not two streams of authority.

Behold now, the goodness and the severity of God. First, He removes Saul's spiritual authority, effectively tearing the kingdom out of his hand and then giving it to someone else. Secondly, He then sends an evil spirit to come upon him to as they say today, 'stress him out.' Saul was filled with anxiety and depression and as a consequence, he became a very ill-tempered man who was given to bouts of rage. The judgment upon him was severe but the Lord didn't take away all His mercies from Saul and God brought a temporary remedy for his suffering. The irony of it all is that the remedy for Saul's troubled spirit was the untroubled spirit of David! The servants of Saul brought this kid in one day to play his harp in an effort to make Saul feel better and nobody realized that this kid was the next king; the next *anointed* king of Israel! *'Oh the depths of the wisdom and knowledge of God! How unsearchable are His judgments and His ways, past finding out!'*

So, from the day of the great switch, when the Spirit of the Lord left Saul and came upon David, Saul was king in outward things only. The real power behind the throne had gone from him. The young minstrel in his house was the true king, and nobody knew it! (Well, nobody except the minstrel.)

Saul's life and tenure of the kingdom became an even sadder story for when the real power behind the throne has left; a man, even though he may still be king, is left with only the framework of executive power. All he has left are the accoutrements of power; the last vestiges of his kingdom.

Saul's crown and Saul's spear were among those sad items for what does the word 'vestige' mean? A vestige is a mark, a trace or visible evidence of something that is no longer present or in existence!

What does a man do when he's lost the wind beneath his wings?

He flaps! He flaps his 'wings' like mad in an effort to convince himself and everyone else that he's still got it!; that he can still fly if he wants to! And if he's a good actor or a good salesman, he'll be able to pull it off for a while but the dark clouds over his kingdom will continue to gather and the results coming in will continue to get worse and worse. Eventually, the true situation will be revealed because *'you can fool all of the people some of the time; you can fool some of the people all of the time; but you can't fool all of the people all of the time!'*

It's at this point where Saul and his spear become an unhealthy partnership. The spear which had been the mystical symbol of his Divine right to command became an extension of his insecurity and his rage. For Saul, his spear, the 'king's spear' still reflected his Divine calling and right to be king and so he took it with him everywhere he went.

Meanwhile, David grew up into a mighty man of valor, having the favor of Saul along with the entire king's family and their servants. Indeed, it seemed that *everyone* in Israel loved David! The people knew how much Saul himself loved David; especially when he exalted him and put him in charge of the nation's military.

Things were going well between them until one day, as David and his men were returning home from a victorious battle with the Philistines that the celebrations turned sour when the women of Israel sang a song about them both. It was the wrong song as far as Saul was concerned, but the women didn't mean it the way he took it. They thought the song no doubt would have pleased him because they knew how much he loved David. Furthermore, the women of Israel didn't come out of the cities to meet David; they came out to meet Saul!

1 Samuel 18:6-12

'Now it happened as they were coming home, when David was returning from the slaughter of the Philistine, that the women had come out of all the cities of Israel, singing and dancing, to meet King Saul, with tambourines, with joy, and with musical instruments.

So the women sang as they danced, and said: "Saul has slain his thousands, and David his ten thousands."

Then Saul was very angry, and the saying displeased him; and he said, "They have ascribed to David ten thousands, and to me they have ascribed only thousands. Now what more can he have but the kingdom?"

So Saul eyed David from that day forward.

And it happened on the next day that the distressing spirit from God came upon Saul, and he prophesied in the house. So David played music with his hand, as at other times; but there was a spear in Saul's hand. And Saul cast the spear, for he said, "I will pin David to the wall!" But David escaped his presence twice.

Now Saul was afraid of David, because the Lord was with him, but had departed from Saul.'

The Enemy called: 'Insecurity'

I think it would be fair to say that the people *respected* Saul but they *loved* David! He had become the 'darling' of the nation and the ironic thing was that the people thought that King Saul was the happiest of everyone about it all. They were wrong. The spear which never left Saul's side became a direct expression of his troubled temperament. His fears, his anxieties and his rage were now the power behind the throne. Another spirit became the driving force of his turbulent personality and his spear gave full expression to his feelings. "I will pin David to the wall!" he said. And he threw the spear at David to kill him –twice!

1 Samuel 19:9-10

'Now the distressing spirit from the Lord came upon Saul as he sat in his house with his spear in his hand. And David was playing music with his hand. Then Saul sought to pin David to the wall with the spear, but he slipped away from Saul's presence; and he drove the spear into the wall. So David fled and escaped that night.'

The same scenario happened all over again. *"Fool me once -shame on you; fool me twice -shame on me!"* When a man crosses the line like this a second time, you've got to leave —and so David ran away for his life.

Jonathan, Saul's son, loved David and he was so upset with what had transpired that he tried his best to bring peace between them both; pleading with his father to accept David. But Saul was 'losing it fast' by this point and he even tried to kill Jonathan the peace-maker one day and once again, it was that spear of his that he used.

1 Samuel 20:32-33

'And Jonathan answered Saul his father, and said to him, "Why should he be killed? What has he done?" Then Saul cast a spear at him to kill him, by which Jonathan knew that it was determined by his father to kill David.'

Saul's anxieties were now dominating him and governing all his behavior.

His spear was always at hand and he became scary to everyone around him. He gathered his troops to go and search for David and he began to pursue him relentlessly. At that point in Saul's life, the only good David was a dead David!)

1 Samuel 22:6

'When Saul heard that David and the men who were with him had been discovered —now Saul was staying in Gibeah under a tamarisk tree in Ramah, with his spear in his hand, and all his servants standing about him.'

There he is again at his place in Gibeon; standing under the shade of a sacred tree with all his soldiers around him and his spear is where it usually is -in his hand. He's ready to go and find David and slay him. There came moments when he would get very close to capturing David but the Lord always intervened and helped David escape. Sometimes, Saul would unwittingly get so close to where David and his men were that he was completely oblivious to the mortal danger he himself was in! On two previous occasions, King Saul had thrown his spear to kill David and it's interesting to note that the Lord gave David two opportunities to slay *him*!

The first of those incidents took place in a cave when Saul stepped into the darkness to privately relieve himself. Unbeknown to Saul was the fact that David and his men were hiding in the recesses of that cave. With their eyes being accustomed to the darkness, they saw that it was the king and they urged David to kill him right there and then; but David restrained himself and his men. The second incident took place when King Saul and his soldiers encamped for the night and they all fell into a deep sleep which allowed David and his nephew Abishai to creep into the camp and stand right next to the sleeping Saul.

1 Samuel 26:7-12

'So David and Abishai came to the people by night; and there Saul lay sleeping within the camp, with his spear stuck in the ground by his head. And Abner and the people lay all around him.

Then Abishai said to David, "God has delivered your enemy into your hand this day. Now therefore, please, let me strike him at once with the spear, right to the earth; and I will not have to strike him a second time!"

But David said to Abishai, "Do not destroy him; for who can stretch out his hand against the Lord's anointed, and be guiltless?"

David said furthermore, "As the Lord lives, the Lord shall strike him, or his day shall come to die, or he shall go out to battle and perish. "The Lord forbid that I should stretch out my hand against the Lord's anointed. But please, take now the spear and the jug of water that are by his head, and let us go."

So David took the spear and the jug of water by Saul's head, and they got away; and no man saw or knew it or awoke. For they were all asleep, because a deep sleep from the Lord had fallen on them.'

David took two things away with him as proof of that moment when once again, he had spared Saul's life. He took the spear of Saul that was stuck in the ground by his head and he took the king's personal water-jug. David, then, from a distance called out to the king and told him how he had spared his life and Saul, to his credit, had a great change of heart towards him.

1 Samuel 26:21-22

'Then Saul said, "I have sinned. Return, my son David. For I will harm you no more, because my life was precious in your eyes this day. Indeed I have played the fool and erred exceedingly."

And David answered and said, "Here is the king's spear. Let one of the young men come over and get it."'

God brought a level of momentary reconciliation between them both and they peacefully went their separate ways. Troubles were still to come to both of them but their personal war with each other was over.

Judgment Day

Time was moving quickly now for Saul and the 'end game' was unfolding. As Saul's life comes to a close and as he and his sons and the army of Israel are facing the prospect of defeat at the hand of the Philistines; he is once again reported to be seen with his spear. Even at the end, Saul and his spear seem to be inseparable. The Philistines had won the battle and they were chasing hard after Saul, shooting him with arrows and severely wounding him. He knew that it was all over but he was still alive and he was afraid of what the Philistines might do to him before he expired. He was dying for sure but not quick enough. Then a young Amalekite who was there at the scene later said that he saw Saul leaning on his spear and at Saul's request, he finished him off.

If his report to David is true, it reveals the sad truth that the very last moment of Saul's life has him leaning on his ever-present spear. He leant on his spear because God was not there to be leaned upon!

Victory is not about the spear. It's about the Lord whose battle it is!

When Joshua raised his spear, God *gave* him the victory because He was *with* him in it. The Spirit of God was upon Joshua *and* his spear! When Saul was God's man in Israel, the Lord was with him *and* his spear; but when the Lord left Saul, all Saul had left was *his* spear. He became like Samson without hair! And when the Spirit of the Lord had left these two men, Samson became like every other man and Saul's spear became like everybody else's spear.

When Goliath of Gath came to defy Israel it was young David who understood these truths when he said to him, *"You come to me with a sword and with a spear, but I come to you in the Name of the Lord of Hosts whom you have defied. I will strike you today so that everyone will know that there is a God in Israel and that they may also know that the Lord does not save or deliver with sword and spear, for the battle is the Lord's and He will give you into our hands!"*

And so it was, with a sling and stone from a young shepherd boy's hand, that the Spirit of God brought Goliath of Gath down to the ground!

Hallelujah! It's not by might nor by power; (by spear) but by My Spirit, says the Lord! A man's right to rule comes from the Spirit of God and not from his weapons of war! (*Might is not always right*). Saul trusted in his weapons. He trusted in his spear and he took it everywhere because it was like a 'security blanket' for him. When the Spirit of the Lord left him, he became a very insecure man and he protected himself with his soldiers around him and with the spear in his hand. He felt better when it was near him; when it was next to him, ready for him to use. The spear gave him his sense of royal command and with it he could dispatch some of his 'problems' and feel right about it in the moment! But through David, the Lord showed him that it could be taken off him at any time should God so desire it.

Abuse of Power

The point of this message is this: We all have things that support our lives and even give us the right to do what we do. God gives us the right and the power to use what He's given to us but if we should ever lose the blessing of God; if we should ever grieve and quench the Spirit of God; we had better watch out! All of us need to be careful in these matters and especially those in ministry positions. A man with the office but without the Spirit of God can easily become a danger to himself as well as others!

The ministry of Christ can become a perilous place because it places great demands upon the Minister's soul; demands that can cause him to react badly sometimes –even when he *does* have the Spirit of God, who is the Spirit of *Grace*. At the end of the day, God is our spear! God is our right and our security. Better to have a sling and five stones *with* God in your life than a sword and spear *without* Him!

So, the questions concerning this matter are these: "What, if anything is the 'spear' in your life? Who or what are *you* leaning on? As a Minister, is your security in your position; in your work, or in the Lord? Are you using your authority and your words as a spear to 'pin people to the wall'? Do you raise your voice every time you feel under attack? Do you hurl accusations back at people? Do you slam doors and have you ever been known to have thrown things at people?

Don't be a Saul with a spear –be a David with a harp!

Playing the Fool

What is a fool? The dictionary describes a fool as a silly or a stupid person. It tells us that a fool is a person who lacks judgment or sense.

In olden times, kings would hire such a person to amuse them. He was known professionally as the 'court fool' or the 'court jester.' His job was to entertain and provide a diversion from the seriousness of life. In a more modern sense, 'to act like a fool' is to make light of serious things; to joke and play around with them. To 'fool around' is to putter around aimlessly or waste time. And in today's understanding, to 'fool around' is to be sexually promiscuous, especially in adultery. To 'fool away' means to spend money unwisely and squander what you have. To 'fool with' means to handle carelessly –like 'you don't fool with a loaded gun' or 'you don't fool with someone's affections.'

So, a fool does foolish things. The Bible has a lot to say about foolish men; foolish women; foolish virgins; foolish people; foolish prophets; foolish shepherds; a foolish nation; a foolish son, etc.

The apostle Paul told us in Ephesians 5 v15 – *"See then that you walk circumspectly, not as fools but as wise."* The Word of God reveals to us that foolishness is found in the heart of the man who says "There is no God." The beginning of foolishness is when you think and when you act like there is no God and therefore there will be no real consequences for what you do. In other words, you're in a whole world of your own making–a make-believe one! And it's not until that 'world' is severely punctured that the fool has any chance of 'waking up' out of it.

I want to take a look at three men in the Bible who all should have known better than to 'play the fool.' Let's look at the first one –King Saul –the Lord's anointed.

The Foolish King

As we have read in the previous chapter, King Saul was a choice young man; head and shoulders above all the rest. He had it all. God gave him the kingdom and made him 'captain over the Lord's inheritance' –His very own people. However, Saul was a disobedient king and he squandered the currency of God's good will towards him. He paid the price of God's favor leaving *him* and resting upon *another* man instead.

That other man was David and Saul recognized the blessings of God upon him and foolishly fought against him. And by so doing, he foolishly fought against God! To fight against the anointing of God on a man to the point of harming him is to shake your fist against Heaven and hurt yourself in the process.

1 Samuel 13:13-14

'And Samuel said to Saul, "You have done foolishly. You have not kept the commandment of the Lord your God, which He commanded you. For now the Lord would have established your kingdom over Israel forever.

But now your kingdom shall not continue. The Lord has sought for Himself a man after His own heart, and the Lord has commanded him to be commander over His people, because you have not kept what the Lord commanded you."

From this moment on, Saul began to say and do foolish things; even to the point of nearly losing his own son Jonathan through a stupid, unnecessary oath that he made his army perform. Then he turned his heart against his son in law David, whom he once loved and began to seek his life, pursuing him from place to place. Day after day, Saul and his army searched the countryside, looking for David and his men but they never found them because God was with David and helped him to escape from their 'nets.' This went on for a long time until God called a halt to it by once again, giving Saul into the hands of David. It all happened one night when David and Abishai stole into the evening camp of Saul and his men. There in the center of all the sleeping bodies they found Saul and while Abishai would have instantly taken Saul's life, David restrained him and walked away with Saul's spear and water-jug to prove where he had actually been. In the morning David stood on the top of a faraway hill and cried out to Abner, the general of Saul's army and Saul recognized the voice of David.

What a moment this was! That day, David gave Saul the shock of his life!

"Is that your voice, my son David?" said Saul.

"It is my voice, my lord, O king" David replied. *"Why does my lord pursue his servant, for what have I done; what evil is in my hand?"*

In that moment, Saul's conscience was laid bare through the kindness of David and wisdom momentarily returned to Saul's heart and mind when he admitted his faults.

1 Samuel 26:21

'Then Saul said, "I have sinned. Return, my son David, because my life was precious in your eyes this day. Indeed I have played the fool and erred exceedingly."'

King Saul had 'played the fool.' One of the evidences that a person is playing the fool is when they act against even their own interests! It was not in Saul's interest to seek the life of David, but his obsessional behavior robbed him of good sense and he 'erred exceedingly.' Chasing David down was one of the biggest mistakes of his life – it was all so unnecessary and he brought anguish to himself and to his own family. He brought strain between himself and his son Jonathan and also with his daughter Michal.

In Saul's make-believe world, he thought that he could take David's life and get away with it. In the world of a 'powerful' fool, only the acceptance of *truth* can bring reality to bear, as it dawns upon a darkened mind.

The beginning of recovery is when the foolish person says, "I have sinned." (The prodigal son's journey to recovery was sealed when he said to his father, "Father, I have sinned, against Heaven and before you.")

That morning, King Saul 'came to himself' and in all sincerity, he asked David to come back home with him.

For the Minister who has a position of authority over his staff and congregation, he must remind himself of the follies of King Saul; making sure that he doesn't copy his behavior by fighting against other anointed Ministers in his life. He must not openly oppose them or seek to undermine them but to be thankful to God for them. To push them away would be to ironically act against his own interests! Eventually, the animosity towards them would be noticed and all manner of distresses would arise, even in those near and dear. Jealousy and rage are killers!

King Saul persecuted the Lord's anointed and consequently his judgement became impaired. He ultimately fought against God and so God frustrated him at every turn. That's what happens when you 'fool around' and handle God's people carelessly.

The Foolish General

Who was Abner? Abner was the general over the armies of King Saul and he was his protector. Abner's rise to power no doubt came as a result of Saul's accession to the throne for Abner was related to Saul. Saul trusted him like no other. Whenever there was a royal banquet, Saul as king would take his place at the top left hand corner next to the wall; his left side and back being shielded by the corner and Abner his general would sit at his right hand to guard him there.

So, Abner's job was two-fold: Command the armies of Israel and guard the king, the Lord's anointed. These things he did but the Scriptures reveal that he had private aspirations of his own. I think that David perceived a propensity for disloyalty in Abner for although it had been a deep sleep from the Lord that had descended upon the camp of Saul that night, David still charged Abner with 'dereliction of duty' towards the king!

1 SAMUEL 26:14–16

'And David called out to the people and to Abner the son of Ner, saying, "Do you not answer Abner?" Then Abner answered and said, "Who are you, calling out to the king?" So David said to Abner, "Are you not a man? And who is like you in Israel? Why

then have you not guarded your lord and king? For one of the people came in to destroy your lord the king.

This thing that you have done is not good. As the Lord lives, you deserve to die, because you have not guarded your master, the Lord's anointed. And now see where the king's spear is, and the jug of water that was by his head."'

Abner was a man of great influence in the kingdom and his position rested upon his whole-hearted devotion to King Saul and the royal family. Yes, he was 'family' himself but he wasn't royalty –but he began to act like he was! This is where Abner and wisdom began to leave one another because his loyalty to the royal family became more and more questionable.

One of Abner's strengths was that he could 'read the moment.' He had 'understanding of the times' and he knew what Israel ought to do but he sought to use the times for his own advantage. You see, Abner began to push himself forward and assume authority that he didn't have. After the death of Saul and some of his sons, he began to take advantage of Ishbosheth, Saul's next son to reign; and slowly but surely he began to tighten his grip on the kingdom.

2 SAMUEL 3:6-12

'Now it was so, while there was war between the house of Saul and the house of David, that Abner was strengthening his hold on the house of Saul. And Saul had a concubine, whose name was Rizpah, the daughter of Aiah. So Ishbosheth said to Abner, "Why have you gone in to my father's concubine?"

The Abner became very angry at the words of Ishbosheth, and said, "Am I a dog's head that belongs to Judah? Today I show loyalty to the house of Saul your father, to his brothers, and to his friends, and have not delivered you into the hand of David; and you charge me today with a fault concerning this woman?

May God do so to Abner, and more also, if I do not do for David as the Lord has sworn to him – to transfer the kingdom from the house of Saul, and set up the throne of David over Israel and over Judah, from Dan to Beersheba." And he could not answer Abner another word, because he feared him.

Then Abner sent messengers on his behalf to David, saying, "Whose is the land?" saying also, "Make your covenant with me, and indeed my hand shall be with you to bring all Israel to you."'

As I said, Abner could read the moment well and he knew the prophecies concerning David and furthermore, he knew that the elders of Israel had in the past, sought for David to be their king. He saw how things were going politically and with a young, inexperienced king on the throne of Israel, Abner strengthened himself in the kingdom. He became emboldened to the point where he would cross royal protocols and take for himself one of the late King Saul's concubines! Abner reached the point where the young King Ishbosheth could have said to his advisors: "What more can he have but the kingdom?"

Abner knew that *he* was the one really in charge. His ambitions were getting the better of him and ultimately he would pay for them with his life. His job description as has been duly noted was to lead the armies of Israel and to guard the king but as he read the proverbial 'writing on the wall' he became increasingly unfaithful to his charge and found it quite easy to switch his loyalties. Abner sought to make David king over all Israel but not without a deal. *"Make your covenant with me"* he said to David, *"and I will bring all Israel to you."* David agreed and sent him away in peace but

Joab, the general of David's armies who was returning to Hebron became alarmed when he discovered that Abner, his opposite number in Israel had been given a feast and had left with a firm understanding from David as to the immediate future.

At this point, everything was working out well for Abner. He would deliver Israel to David by effectively becoming the new 'king-maker' and then continue to be a mighty man and a prince in Israel. Joab, the general of David's army had different ideas. Still seething from his brother's death by the hand of Abner, he and his other brother Abishai schemed to bring Abner back to Hebron and then, taking him aside privately, they slew him.

Abner's calling was to be a 'hedge' around the king of Israel. He betrayed his king and by so doing, he broke down the 'hedge of his own integrity' and as the Scriptures say: *'He who breaks down a hedge, a serpent will get in and bite him.'* (KJV)

As a prince and a great man in Israel, Abner should have finished his course and should have been buried with honor but as David lamented over his murder, he could only ask the rhetorical question: *"Died Abner as a fool dies?"* 'Abner -died like a common man who perished at the hands of wicked men' was his obituary. He was a prince and a great man who died a fool's death! Abner 'played the fool' when he sold his loyalty to enhance his own ambitions. He forgot that there was a God in Israel. He forgot that there was a Heavenly king-maker. By pushing himself forward, he despised the authority that God had given to Saul and his family and he assumed too much concerning himself.

What Abner tried to do has been foolishly repeated many times over when even the people of God have thought more highly of themselves than they ought to think. This scenario plays out often in the Ministry today; when so-called 'people of influence' in a congregation assume too much and begin to push themselves forward at the expense of the leadership. With secret conversations and even petitions, they assume a 'king-maker' role in the church and many are sadly taken with their persuasive words. People who do this 'err exceedingly' and the Lord has to come and preserve His anointing by preserving His Minister. Over the years, God has had to discipline some 'good people' when they have wittingly or unwittingly strengthened their own hands against the Lord's anointed.

The Foolish Minister

Everybody it seems remembers the fateful Delilah and how she eventually brought the mighty Samson down but there was a path that led to that dreadful moment in his life and ministry. The Word of God tells us to take heed to ourselves even to the point of disciplining our bodies so that having preached to others we should not become disqualified ourselves!

Proverbs 4:25-27

'Let your eyes look straight ahead, and your eyelids look right before you. Ponder the path of your feet, and let all your ways be established. Do not turn to the right or the left; remove your foot from evil.'

Samson was a man who was chosen by God before he was born. He was dedicated to the Lord as an infant and he grew up devoted to God and to His service. Added to that was a special gift of the Holy Spirit upon his life which for kingdom purposes gave him incredible strength against the enemy. Samson however did not continue in that spirit of consecration and his problem, like it has been for many men -was women.

Long before he began to visit other women, he had difficulty coping with his wife, who manipulated him through tears and accusations, saying "You only hate me! You do not love me!" He thought that he could handle her, but when she pressed him to explain the riddle that he had told her people, he relented.

Judges 16:1-3

'Now Samson went to Gaza and saw a harlot there, and went in to her. When the Gazites were told, "Samson has come here!" they surrounded the place and lay in wait for him all night at the gate of the city. They were quiet all night, saying, "In the morning, when it is daylight, we will kill him."

And Samson lay low till midnight; then he arose at midnight, took hold of the doors of the gate of the city and the two gate-posts, pulled them up, bar and all, put them on his shoulders, and carried them to the top of the hill that faces Hebron.'

Here is one of the mysteries of the ministry of God in that His power can still flow even when the Minister himself is not living right. In every Minister that falls to sexual sin, there always seems to be a period of time when the *blessings upon* his life are operating concurrently with the *sins in* his life. He can fool himself into thinking that God is alright with the situation but history reveals the sad truth that it's only a matter of time before everything unravels. It seems to be a universal truth: that which is done in *'the inner rooms will eventually be proclaimed on the housetops.'*

Here we have Samson 'fooling around' in the modern sense of the phrase and because the 'tap of grace' hasn't been completely turned off he becomes quite comfortable in his sinful activities. He is now visiting prostitutes and he still thinks that he can manage everything but he hasn't accounted for a woman like Delilah! Delilah is 'waiting in the wings' and she *will* bring him down. Because Samson has 'played the fool' for so long, he doesn't understand that God in His mercy has been giving him time to repent and he doesn't appreciate the precarious nature of his true position before God. He doesn't perceive the imminent danger that's ready to destroy his life and ministry. Like a foolish man that builds his house upon the sand, in the end, it all comes crashing down and everybody hears the noise that it makes.

Delilah eventually came into his life. How they met we do not know but we do know that they had a tenuous relationship especially over the issue of the secret of his unusual power. Delilah began to enquire of him as to the source of his great strength and with a cavalier attitude, he began to toy with her and fool with her emotions. Just like his wife, she too pressed him in similar ways to tell her the secret, saying to him, "How can you say 'I love you' when your heart is not with me?" She pressed him every day about this matter and she tormented him with her words and he eventually gave in to her demands.

Samson had played with fire! He'd 'fooled with' the anointing of God; revealing the mystery of his strength to a woman who destroyed his ministry as she lulled him to sleep on her knees. The Philistines came and shaved off the seven locks of his hair and the strength of his covenant with God was gone in an instant. He woke up from his sleep and he thought he would carry on as normal, only to find out to his horror that the Spirit of the Lord had left him. His strength was gone. Samson 'played the fool' and in the end, Delilah 'took him for a fool.'

And so it is with many Ministers who 'fool around' and fall into sexual sin; the day comes when the 'house' comes crashing down. In such cases the phrase 'fooling around' does no real justice to describe the complete devastation that such sinfulness brings to the Minister and his family as well as the church and the Body of Christ in general.

In a conversation with a high-ranking Minister who for his denomination had to help restore Ministers who had committed moral failure; he told me that in his interviews with them, he discovered that they all had the same basic thought process that allowed them to do what they did. He told me that they all sincerely believed that they were special to God and because of that; they thought that God would understand their unique situation. They all said that they knew what they were doing was wrong but they all thought that God would make an exception for them! How shocking it must be for such people when the 'rod of rebuke' comes down upon them! Like Samson, they've woken up but the damage has been done!

So, there you have it. Saul 'played the fool' by fighting the anointing of God in a subordinate. Abner 'played the fool' by betraying the anointing of his leader and Samson 'played the fool' by diminishing the anointing of God through sinful behavior. All three of them forgot that they were handling 'hot coals of fire' and they all paid dearly. God loved them all but His holiness demanded their respect and His Spirit could not and would not make an exception for them no matter how special they thought they were! Their make-believe worlds caused them to lose the 'fear of the Lord' and spiritual reality became the first casualty in the battle for their souls. They became like those who were described in the New Testament as *'professing themselves to be wise, they became fools.'*

Let us all hear the words of the apostle Paul again when he said, *"Let us walk circumspectly, not as fools but as wise."*

Tell it not in Gath

What do we do when things have gone badly wrong for us? What do we do when the things that have gone wrong pertain to God and to the Ministry? This chapter is about moments such as these and hopefully it will teach us how to rightly handle bad news if and when it comes.

1 Samuel 31:1-6

'Now the Philistines fought against Israel; and the men of Israel fled from before the Philistines, and fell slain on Mount Gilboa. Then the Philistines followed hard after Saul and his sons. And the Philistines killed Jonathan, Abinadab, and Malchishua, Saul's sons.

The battle became fierce against Saul. The archers hit him, and he was severely wounded by the archers. Then Saul said to his armorbearer, "Draw your sword, and thrust me through with it, lest these uncircumcised men come and thrust me through and abuse me." But his armorbearer would not, for he was greatly afraid. Therefore Saul took a sword, and fell on it. And when his armorbearer saw that Saul was dead, he also fell on his sword, and died with him.

So Saul, his three sons, his armorbearer, and all his men died together that same day.'

The end of an era had come. That which had existed for forty years was now over. The king was dead. Saul, the son of Kish, the king of Israel had been slain in battle. And not him alone, but his three valiant princes perished with him; the beloved Jonathan being one of them! Surrounding Saul's dead body were his sons, his armorbearer and the remnants of his army. What a scene! What a mess! There on Mount Gilboa lies the flower of the royal household in blood! The king of Israel, full of arrows and a sword sticking out of his back; his spear lying next to him; his shield flung somewhere in the vicinity near his empty chariot –this is the scene that the Philistines discovered the following day.

The time of judgment had arrived. For countless sins, including the massacre of the priests and their families at Nob, Saul had been placed under the 'sword of the Lord.' The warnings from the Lord were long over. It had been some time since the Lord had spoken to Saul. God had forsaken him and He didn't answer him anymore. Perpetual disobedience and grievous personal attacks on his son-in-law David, even to the point of giving his wife to another man, had brought Saul to this dreadful moment.

There were no more directive dreams from God and no more revelations of God through any of the prophets; all of which resulted in him seeking spiritual guidance through a medium. Indeed, Saul had entered the 'dead zone' with God and his departure from this life was at hand. It was 'change-over' time in the kingdom, for the Lord had now become Saul's enemy. That day, on the mountains of Gilboa, the Lord tore the kingdom from out of Saul's hand and in the Spirit, gave it to David. The king indeed was dead.

2 Samuel 1:17-27

'Then David lamented with this lamentation over Saul and over Jonathan his son, and he told them to teach the children of Judah the Song of the Bow; indeed it is written in the Book of Jasher:

"The beauty of Israel is slain on your high places! How the mighty have fallen! Tell it not in Gath, proclaim it not in the streets of Ashkelon – lest the daughters of the Philistines rejoice, lest the daughters of the uncircumcised triumph. O mountains of Gilboa, let there be no dew nor rain upon you, nor fields of offerings. For the shield of the mighty is cast away there! The shield of Saul, not anointed with oil, from the blood of the slain, from the fat of the mighty, the bow of Jonathan did not turn back, and the sword of Saul did not return empty.

Saul and Jonathan were beloved and pleasant in their lives, and in their death they were not divided; They were swifter than eagles, they were stronger than lions. O daughters of Israel, weep over Saul, who clothed you in scarlet, with luxury; who put ornaments of gold on your apparel.

How the mighty have fallen in the midst of battle! Jonathan was slain in your high places. I am distressed for you, my brother Jonathan; You have been very pleasant to me; Your love to me was wonderful, surpassing the love of women. How the mighty have fallen, and the weapons of war perished!"'

How the Mighty have Fallen!

Here is one of the greatest eulogies ever spoken! It is rich in sentiment and in content but the glory of this eulogy stems from the man who spoke it. The man who gave this funeral oration was none other than the oppressed son-in-law himself! Observe the magnanimous nature of David as he speaks respectfully of a man who had been an absolute 'nightmare' to him! What is also worth noting is the fact that when David gave this eulogy, he was still a relatively young man. Clearly, David was a young man with an excellent spirit! There was nothing in David's heart that would have seized this moment as an opportunity to tell everyone around him, "I told you so!" or "He had it coming!" But such was the heart of David that instead of denigrating the memory of Saul, he chose to remember the good things. He chose to refer to Saul as the 'beauty of Israel' and he dwelt on Saul's past victories when both Saul and his son Jonathan were valiant in battle. He preferred to remind the women in Israel that they had all enjoyed prosperity under Saul's reign and had been able to clothe themselves in the finest materials. They had put on ornaments of gold and had been no strangers to luxury.

Simply put, David didn't revenge himself on a dead man's memory but rather concealed his faults. Many of King Saul's mistakes would have been public knowledge by then but David didn't include them in his eulogy.

(Love teaches us to be charitable with someone's memory and wisdom teaches us to say nothing bad about the dead. Here is a lesson for any Minister who has to officiate at a funeral –speak about the good and not about the bad. Only make sure that all your commendations are true for if you give praise where it isn't warranted, you will discredit yourself and your words will sound hollow.)

The Beauty of Israel

What was David doing here? In sincerity, he was making the best of a bad situation. It was a dreadful moment in the country. The people of God were thrown into a crisis and it's precisely those kinds of moments that need a 'David' to 'steady the ship' and give folks a sense that they'll all make it through. The nation now had a dynasty under judgment and its king, the 'beauty of Israel' lay dead in a blood-stained heap upon the mountains. David's words spoke into the darkness of that moment as the Spirit of grace was poured into his lips.

The truth was that God had done all this. It was the Lord who had removed Saul because his sins had reached such a 'boiling point' with God that He regretted making him king. And so this huge man, this colossus of a figure-head had now been cut down to the ground. He who had once served the Lord and advanced the cause of God so well had now just become a memory. "How the mighty have fallen!" David lamented. That was David's response but what would be his advice?

Tell it not in Gath

'Tell it not in Gath, proclaim it not in the streets of Ashkelon –lest the daughters of the Philistines rejoice, lest the daughters of the uncircumcised triumph.'

That was David's advice. Tell it not in Gath and proclaim it not in Ashkelon. What David was saying was "Don't give the enemies of God this news!" He was saying by these words: "Let's not make this situation any worse than it already is!" He knew that the demise of Saul and his sons would have caused the Philistines to revel in it all and gloat over them with scorn.

(Unfortunately, David himself would forget this point when later in his life he would commit his own dark sins in the matter of Bathsheba and her husband. He would also come under the judgment of God for the despicable things he had done and how he had given the enemies of God a great advantage. The prophet Nathan said to David at that time: *"By this deed, you have given great occasion to the enemies of the Lord to blaspheme."*)

Let us *all* walk carefully before the Lord and if a Minister of Christ wrecks his life and ministry –tell it not in Gath! If he has subverted righteousness and has been caught with his fingers 'in the till' with the treasury of the church having been robbed –tell it not in Gath! If he has trapped himself in an immoral affair and God has blown the 'lid of secrecy' right off –tell it not in Gath! The enemies of the Lord will certainly find out, but let us not add further measure to the news! Let us not put even more 'fuel on the fire' for the news will travel fast enough and it doesn't need our 'help.' The enemy will come to strip the 'slain' and find the carcass of a broken man and endeavor to pin him like a trophy on the 'front page' of a wall in their city. They will quickly decapitate him from all the good that he ever did and rejoice in his failure and gloat over his demise. Not once will they really take into consideration the pain it has brought to the people who love him and who have sought to stand by him.

Damage Limitation

When these things happen, and happen they will; let us not exacerbate the situation any further. When leadership is judged, even if it has been oppressive to us like it was in David's case, let us try and keep the matter 'in-house.' Tell it not to the media! Proclaim or publish it not, but let us minimize the damage it has caused as much as possible. Let us not be found guilty of malicious gossip however 'juicy' the information might be!

This is not a 'hiding of sin' or a cover-up of immorality. We're talking about a situation which God has already exposed and the truth is now out. In these circumstances we must 'buy the truth and sell it not.' We must buy the sad events; learn from them and by the grace of God, never repeat them! We have a duty to limit the damage and protect the 'lambs' in the Body of Christ. We have an obligation to watch over the flock and guard the 'Israel of God' with our lives.

Judgment for sin will always come and if the soul in question is still alive, there must be repentance and a loving road of recovery made available to them. It's a long, hard road for all concerned but the Lord's grace can re-enter the Minister's life once again and complete restoration can be enjoyed by all those involved.

So, when these things happen, let's not feed the enemy. Let's not give extra information to the Philistines who hate both us and our God. Let us not be careless with our news. Tell it *not* in Gath!

The Secrets of God

In one of my recent sermons I was talking about Moses being drawn by his curiosity to the burning bush and then when God saw that he drew nigh; He began to call to him out of the bush, but then warned him not to come too close. Moses was to approach God but at the same time, keep a healthy distance. As one man once put it; *'God called Moses to draw nigh but not so as to pry.'*

To 'pry' is to enquire impertinently. Impertinence is a word that describes intrusive or presumptuous actions. Impertinence is rude, brash, insolent behavior. It comes from the Latin word 'impertinens' which means 'not belonging.' So, an impertinent person is someone who pries or intrudes into an area that does not 'belong to them.' I'm afraid that these are words that well-describe our generation. It is full of fresh, bold, arrogant people both young and old who believe that the rules are for everybody else and not for them! That's how we can have couples turn up at the Whitehouse for a dinner-party that they were never invited to! Impertinence! It is the height of impertinence for anyone to make an appearance at a Presidential function without first receiving an invitation. We call this 'gate-crashing.'

In this final chapter, I'd like to address this spirit that's in more hearts than it should be; and yes, that includes us –the Christians.

I think that we can all agree that God has been generous to us beyond belief and that He has revealed so much of Himself through Jesus His Living Word and though the Bible, His Written Word. However, God has retained some things that are personal to Him. You will find in your life as a Christian that God has some 'no-go areas' where the only navigational instruments you have lie in the area of trust. However, we can all be assured that if God hasn't revealed something to us that it will be for our ultimate benefit.

Think about it. We don't tell our children everything do we? No, because certain things and certain pieces of information will be too much for them. In fact, if we're not careful, we could easily damage our children if we tell them too much too soon. Children are to develop in a world of innocence for as long as they can, and *then* the veil is taken away, hopefully by degrees and not all at once!

So, let's take a look at this 'spirit of impertinence' and see what it does.

The spirit of Impertinence

This 'spirit' is linked to our egos and it will drive us to want to know everything, immediately. It causes us to live our lives on a continual 'need to know' basis and we cannot rest until we know everything - even things that are not even ours to know! This thing runs deep within many of us. Our mother Eve didn't do very well with this and she received an 'F' for a 'fail.' She was tempted to feel unfulfilled within the world that God had blessed her with and then she was seduced to pry into areas not belonging to her that God said would be deeply damaging. She had everything, yet she wanted more. She began in her heart to *intrude* into things that were not hers, but were God's. Her behavior was as you know, inappropriate and her husband fared no better!

The point that I'm making is this: God has things of His own. Why can't we respect that? There are things He's kept to Himself because He holds the Divine prerogative to do so and because those things are usually kept secret for our benefit! Knowledge does not *always* serve us! Once you know something, you can't un-know it! Your eyes have been opened and there's no going back to the innocence you once stood in.

So let us draw *nigh* to God but let us not *pry* into the secrets that belong to Him; for I'm sure that He would reveal them to us if we really needed to know.

Deuteronomy 29:29

'The secret things belong to the Lord our God, but those things which are revealed belong to us and to our children forever, that we may do all the words of this law.'

So, with God, there are things that are secret and there are things that are revealed. God has blended both the 'hidden' and the 'open' so that together they help us fulfill His laws and walk in His ways.

I want to take a look at three areas that God has largely kept secret from us and in my view; they are clearly for our benefit.

Hidden Spirits

The first area I want to look at is the world of angels and demons. God has revealed quite a lot of that dimension to us so we can safely conclude that He wants us to know at least *some* things about that invisible world. But there's still a veil of mystery surrounding the spirit world. For example, the Scriptures reveal the nature and activity of demons, yet it remains quite silent as to their origins. There may be some Biblical nuances concerning a world before Adam but it remains as conjecture. (Conjecture is an opinion or a theory that lacks sufficient evidence of proof. It's called 'guess-work.')

Angels we know are real. Again, we know a lot about their nature and their activities but God in His wisdom has chosen not to reveal their names to us apart from Michael the archangel and Gabriel –the one who stands in the Presence of God.

Judges 13:17-18

'Then Manoah said to the Angel of the Lord, "What is Your name, that when Your words come to pass we may honor You?"

And the Angel of the Lord said to him, "Why do you ask My name, seeing it is wonderful?"

Another Hebrew word that matches *'wonderful'* is the word *'secret.'*

Down through the centuries and still to-day, many people have been enamored by angels. The pagans have had their 'spirit-guides' and the Christians have had their 'saints' and 'angels.' They have sought to know their names and have their particular presence and activity in their lives. The apostle Paul warned the church in his day to abstain from this.

Colossians 2:18-19

'Let no one cheat you of your reward, taking delight in false humility and worship of angels, intruding into those things which

he has not seen, vainly puffed up by his fleshly mind, and not holding fast to the Head, from whom all the body, nourished and knit together by joints and ligaments, grows with the increase that is from God.'

True spiritual growth comes when you hold Christ as the Head of your life.

Paul is saying that there are some who've bypassed Jesus for angels and they have *intruded* into those things that God has not opened up! In fact, much of it is a deception of the mind and so a walk through this life with *named* angels is a 'make-believe' world of the religious mind. If God then has deliberately withheld the names of angels and kept them secret; kept them wonderful; best not to pry! It's best not to intrude into *those* things. Let the door of 'angel naming' remain shut! This is not to negate the fact that angels *are* with us but let us always remember that the Bible tells us *'that our fellowship is with the Father and the Son.'* Our communication is with them through the Holy Spirit.

Hidden Dates

Another thing that God has kept secret is the day and the hour of Christ's return. God *is* going to send His Son back to this world as King of kings and Lord of lords but the timing of that event is sealed. So, we can safely conclude that the setting of dates to pin-point the return of Christ is futile. That knowledge belongs to God and therefore it is a 'no-go area' for us.

Now, some to-day know that 'naming the date' is pointless, but they're still having a shot at this by stating that Christ will come on a certain Jewish Feast. Who knows? Maybe Jesus will return on a Jewish Feast day. It would certainly fit Biblical patterns if He did; but again, it's just conjecture. It's still in the realm of guess-work and I think that we should stop trying to get a handle on this future, cosmic event and let God have all the glory. *'For in such an hour as you think not, the Son of Man will come.'* Again, Jesus said, *"But of that day and hour, no one knows, not even the angels of heaven, nor the Son, but the Father only!"* Jesus said to His disciples and He says it to us in our day, *"It is not for you to know, the times and the seasons which the Father has put in His own authority."*

Can we accept that? Can we say out loud, "It is not for ME to know?"

Hidden Names

Let me share one more thing that God will keep secret to Himself. I find that this one is the most moving of all because it's based on His personal intimacy with every one of His children.

Revelation 2:17

"He who has an ear, let him hear what the Spirit says to the churches. To him who overcomes I will give some of the hidden manna to eat. And I will give him a white stone, and on the stone a new name written which no one knows except him who receives it."

Here God is promising the one who overcomes a portion of the eternal 'Bread of Life' that will ensure his sustenance in God forever. Added to that will be the gift of a new name written on a white stone which will mark them as a distinct and unique child of God. It will be a deeply personal thing because that new name will be known known *only* to them and to the Lord who gave it to them. In the Old Testament, it was prophesied that Jesus would be called, 'Wonderful,

Counselor, Mighty God, Prince of peace, Everlasting Father.' As Captain of our salvation, He has brought many sons to glory and as the Everlasting Father He will name all His born-again children. This intimacy between the child of God and the Lord Jesus will be something that they uniquely share. How wonderful to know that among the countless numbers of people in heaven, He will know us intimately and even in a City of Divine light, there can remain some beautiful, private things between us and our God! The marvelous thing is that the Lord Jesus also will enjoy such a distinction from *His* Father.

Revelation 19:11-13

'Now I saw heaven opened, and behold, a white horse. And He who sat on him was called Faithful and True, and in righteousness He judges and makes war. His eyes were like a flame of fire, and on His head were many crowns. He had a name written that no one knew except Himself.

He was clothed with a robe dipped in blood, and His name is called The Word of God.'

God the Father will write on Him a name that is deeply personal to them both. Heaven will be full of saved people; full of adopted sons, but there'll be nobody like Jesus, the only begotten Son of God and the Savior of us all. He too will continue to live in the intimacy of His Father's love for once again; the Word will be *with* God.

To Reveal or not to Reveal

So, you can see that in the past, in the present and in the future, God has had and still has the prerogative to reveal or not to reveal. And He knows best!

This is the conclusion that Job came to. If anyone had the mystery of God's will play out in his life, it was Job. When you know what terrible things happened to him, who can blame him for having more questions than answers? Both he and his friends were trying to get to the bottom of it all; trying to understand what was happening; trying to get a handle on those dreadful events, but when God did reveal Himself to Job, he could only reply, *"I have spoken about things that I did not understand; things too wonderful for me, which I did not know."*

I believe that the main reason the book of Job is in the Bible is not to speak to the sinner but to the saint! It's there to speak to the human part of a believer when that 'need to know' part of us erupts to the surface; when we feel that we have the right to know what's going on. Many Christians nowadays believe that they can almost demand God to explain Himself! If that is not impertinence, I don't know what is!

The experience of Job tells us something very important. It tells us that God is not under any obligation to explain things and give us the answers we're looking for! Sometimes, our familiarity with God causes us to be rude with Him and we forget Who He is and what we are!

'Who are we to reply against God? "Shall the thing created say to him who created it, "Why have you made me like this? Does not the potter have power over the clay?"'

"Privacy Please!"

We have to accept the fact that God has His secrets and we can be assured that if He doesn't reveal them, it'll be for our ultimate benefit.

Let God have His things. Is it right for us to intrude into *His* privacy?

In recent days, there has been an outcry in many countries because national security agencies have been found to have gained intrusive access into people's lives. We now know that government intelligence agencies have been reading our mail, listening to our calls, photographing us from lamp-posts and even trash cans! We don't like it! We don't like it one bit! Why don't we like it? It's because they are *invading* our privacy. Most people accept that a certain amount of information-seeking is now necessary for national security. They accept that the intelligence community must draw nigh, but not so as to pry! It's the prying that makes people afraid; wondering if they're being watched in their own homes through their computers and their television sets.

The spirit of this generation allows for a high level of impertinence that intrudes into people's lives inappropriately and our technology and our science are running faster than our ethics and subsequent values. All this information that comes to us to-day does not necessarily benefit us and the negative side of information is affecting our children. In some cases it is allowing them to know far too much far too soon!

Brothers and sisters in Christ; we as the children of God who have been saved by a loving Savior and have come to know a perfect God; we don't need to know every small detail. We walk by faith. We put our *trust* in Him.

We *know* the Potter. We might not know all the details of what He's doing but we know His hands! We recognize His handiwork. Let God be God! Let Him have His privacy. He calls us to draw nigh, but not to pry! Trust Him; He knows what He's doing. Praise Him when He speaks and praise Him when He doesn't! Thank Him when He reveals something and thank Him when He doesn't. Again, God knows best!

The secret things belong to the Lord, but the things that are revealed, belong to us and our children. The Lord giveth; the Lord taketh away. Blessed be the Name of the Lord!

Closing Thoughts

I trust that the chapters throughout this book have been a blessing to your spiritual life and to your ministry. I have endeavored to bring to your heart and mind the sanctity of the ministry of God; with the first seven chapters on 'how it should be' and the remaining seven chapters on 'what to watch out for'!

Underlying all the chapters' runs the theme of 'hot coals of fire' for this is the term that I have chosen to adequately describe the awesome realities of ministering for God, in both Old and New Testament settings.

I have tried to highlight the ignorance that many have when it comes to handling Divine things and I have sought to educate Christian Ministers whose backgrounds have been rooted in the western world; how that the 'spirit of man' ignited by all things Greek, has exalted itself even in the Church.

It has been an alarming thing to observe that within the spiritual fabric of our western culture, that the 'Woman' whose names are 'Mystery, Babylon' has continued to seduce men to reject or ignore the Holy Spirit and His authority over the 'things of Christ.' The word of the Lord to us regarding her is similar to the message He gave Abraham concerning

Hagar and Ishmael: *"Cast out the bondwoman and her son, for the son of the bondwoman shall not be heir with the son of the free woman. So then, brethren, we are not children of the bondwoman but of the free."*

Simply put, to replace, relegate or banish the Person and office of the Holy Spirit is tantamount to serving the 'spirit of this world' –if not in heart, most certainly in practice.

I wrote this book not just to warn Ministers but to encourage them to fulfill the Divine calling upon their lives by living a sanctified life. The chapters herein are meant to stimulate the desires that God has put in their hearts to serve Him. I also wanted to encourage any would-be Minister who has decided in his heart to stay on the side-lines of ministry so as to avoid its restrictions and expectations. To them I say, "Don't wait any longer! Great rewards await those who serve God as a Minister of Christ -in this life and in the next!"

Over all, the burden on my heart to write this book came from a genuine desire to help those already engaged in the work of the ministry; to make them aware that they stand on holy ground before a fire that doesn't extinguish; and that the rewards for service and the price for failure are high.

Ought these things not to be so if we live under the shadow of the Almighty and we speak as the oracles of God?

"Brethren, the grace of our Lord Jesus Christ be with your spirit. Amen."